First Self-Publication I
© Gordo

CW01494910

The right of Gordon Woods to ̶ ̶ ̶ ̶ ̶ ̶ ̶as tne Author of this
work has been asserted by him in accordance with the
Copyright, Design, and Patents Act 1988

Typesetting, layout and design by Artier Design
ISBN: 9798392998098   **Imprint:** Independently published.

Thanks to my children who supported me throughout my disclosures,
that support was instrumental in my success.
Craig Woods, Victoria Woods, Briana (Kanna) Woods
"Nothing is out of your reach".

Foreword

Having followed Gordon on Twitter and read about the sexual abuse he endured at the hands of Celtic Boys' Club founder Jim Torbett; I quietly cheered him on as he fought for justice. *Of course, there is never really justice when you consider the life-long trauma and hidden scars that being sexually abused as a child leaves you with.* Gordon's experience is a dark one, now coming to light and proving that it doesn't matter how old you are, a voice that can highlight this often "hidden" topic can deliver the right outcome and with-it, justice.

It was an honour for me to be asked by Gordon to read his book, "Being Put Through Hoops" - something that really helped me understand more of what this young excited and aspiring football player was experiencing because of his passion. Sadly, this is something I hear regularly from other survivors of Child Sexual Abuse keen to excel in the sporting industry. It's completely upsetting to think that anyone would treat a child in this way, but as I know from my own work – this is an all-too-common reality.

I understood a lot of what Gordon wrote about, especially how the grooming side of being sexually abused is played out including the manipulation, fear and shame that follow - and of course the silence. I have no doubt this read will be inspiring for many, and for me it has been a continued encouragement for my own campaigning.

Gordon's experiences borne out of being sexually abused as a child, through to the legal side of his battle as an adult, results in such a credible author.

What an honour it is to be able to write this foreword' and to be able to do this for someone who I understand, relate to and champion. I appreciate Gordon's story, the difficulties he faced and the grim and dark reality that being sexually abused as a child means. But I also know how powerful the journey can be, especially if you can amplify your story in a way that helps to reduce child sexual abuse, remove the stigmas attached to the conversation and give hope to others.

On a personal note, I began campaigning in 2018, when my own book; Don't Hold Back was published. During these years I have spent much of my time supporting CSA survivors and campaigning against child sexual abuse. In 2023 I created the #NotMyShame movement and have been humbled to connect with many survivors and allies across the world, willing to support the silence of child sexual abuse, turning the tables on a very difficult and dark conversation.

Before you read 'Being Put Through Hoops', I urge you to look at the back cover, at Gordon. A man who has lived with deep scars and silent pain. Because of Gordon, I have no doubt that this read will provide hope, confidence, and support to those suffering in similar silence, and bound by shame.

Emma-Jane Taylor
Author of Don't Hold Back
Campaigner and creator of the #NotMyShame movement
Founder of the charity, Project 90/10

I thank you for your support.
It means a great deal to me personally,
and to all survivors of C.S.A.

Celtic Officials: Jock Stein, Bob Kelly, Jim Torbett, Joe McBride,
Billy McNeil, and Gordon Woods (Front Right)

As you read it will become obvious that I'm not an author, my command of the English language at times will be questioned and probably rightly so. I did not want my words to be written by anyone but me, altered by editing, proof-reading, or sanitisation. I self-published because I refused to allow a third party to instruct me on what I could and could not say, this is my truth. These are all my words, as I spoke to myself, I typed, and this is the result, every word is my own in telling my story. Please forgive any spelling or grammatical errors and the fact there are times when I probably repeat myself.
Better to tell you twice than not at all!

Chapter   *Page*

I thank you sincerely for reading this book and hopefully when you are finished you will appreciate how and why abuse victims have a cloak of darkness throughout their lives. Speaking out assists in removing that darkness and I thank you for helping me speak out.

Due to time and space constraints on media my story wasn't being heard as fully as it should be. A book of my total experience from child to pensioner was the way forward to educate those who needed educated, perhaps even those who don't want to be educated.

My book will relay who I was as a child, my dreams and aspirations before the abuse, and the innocence I had at that time. It details my time at Celtic Boys' Club, and it will clarify some issues that until now have been mired with inaccuracies and confusion.

The book will further explain how my abuse threw me into a life of compunction, self-harm, alcohol, serious crime, and an inability to love my own children as I should have been allowed to do.

It involves the sadness when my parents passed, probably still pained by the guilt they felt at what had happened to me and when the time to talk with them about it all, was cruelly taken away.

"Predators work alone, they work in groups, predators, tragically, know how to remain invisible to everyone other than their poor child victims. Predators are professional paedophiles. Whilst authorities take an amateur approach in outing them our children will always be in danger." © Gordon Woods – 2023

"The scale of paedophilia from the 1960s all the way through to the 1990s was on a scale that I have not seen in any other setting whether that is in relation to sport, or private schools, or anywhere else. A paedophile ring operated at the heart of Celtic Boys' Club for more than 30 years".

The Case Against Celtic Boys Club Podcast,
Patrick McGuire, Senior Lawyer for the victims,
Thompson Solicitors 26th June 2023

Current state of legal actions • July 2023

"Can you imagine if you had 30 former players of Manchester Utd, Barcelona, the LA Lakers, the New York Yankees, and let's be clear, there's far more survivors out there, I have no doubt about that, I'm clear that the 30 brave men who are part of this litigation are the tip of the iceberg. I've no doubt that what we're looking at here, is the biggest, and the most rotten form of child abuse in the entire history of sport".

The Case Against Celtic Boys Club Podcast,
Patrick McGuire, Senior Lawyer for the victims,
Thompson Solicitors 26th June 2023

1. A CHILD AWAITS

I was an ordinary Glasgow kid. Well, at least I thought I was. I played 'Kerbie', 'Kick-the-Can', football, caught bees in jam jars then smashed the jar running away, sometimes not as fast as the bees could fly, unfortunately. I had even begun an interest in the girls at school, I played truant on many occasions from the age of 12 and used to enjoy harassing my parents by doing a disappearing act. Many times, I ran away from home, overnight, only to be apprehended by the police and returned to an irate family. I only got as far as Helensburgh, Airdrie, and Clydebank to name a few but that would change a few years later when I had to be returned home from California... Santa Monica, Los Angeles to be precise, as a runaway 16-year-old!

These were not (as you will read later) the only times I would experience the police being involved in my life. On these early occasions they were always understanding to me. I can recall one or two trying to gently question me as to why I was finding it necessary to continually run away. They obviously were concerned that something was not quite right at home but doubt they had any authority to take it further. Their involvement was soon to change and the lead up to my 'life of crime' had started its journey.

Being born in Clydebank and as a young child, I

think about 4 years old moving to Drumchapel didn't give me a start in life that would have been envied by many. Drumchapel was at that time a fairly new housing estate, all council housing that was intended to be occupied by those who were displaced with the clearance of the Gorbals and other unsavoury locations. Our own particular house was the envy however of many of the other Drumchapel residents. My parents had been fortunate enough to be offered a three-bedroom terraced property rather than one of the 6 or 8 flats to a unit that was available throughout the scheme. We even had stairs and our own back and front door that you didn't need to access through the 'close'. Only 6 houses occupied the terrace and to the right, left, and back of the property we had an abundance of green space ideal for climbing up and falling from trees.

Directly opposite was another large green space that was later to be built on in the form of Waverley Secondary School. The school I would later attend from the age of 12 until I was 15. My home being directly opposite played havoc with my truancy but the kids in Drumchapel learned quickly how to avoid the surveillance of parents and other adults in authority. The houses had originally been built apparently and reserved for local police officers but due to a reduction in staffing levels in Drumchapel Police Station, they reverted to general public occupancy.

My truancy got worse, I remember once, probably at 14 or 15, I was in Glasgow City Centre playing truant and headed up Buchanan Street to catch the bus back to Drumchapel from the terminus in Renfrew Street in time for the school coming out at 4 p.m. As I reached the top of Buchanan Street, Bob Crampsey stuck a microphone in my face with a T.V. Crew in attendance. Jim Baxter had just re-signed for Rangers Football Club, and they were asking the public their views on that breaking news story. Immediately I realised that if this was going to be on the news I was in deep trouble and would be caught out playing truant. I hatched my plan in seconds, "I think he's a cunt" I replied, knowing full well that would never be shown on STV, let alone the BBC! I proceeded up to the bus terminal so proud of myself for having avoided capture.

At 12-years-old I had dreams and aspirations that most kids have but mine was different. I was reaching for the stars, being an R.A.F. Pilot, an Author or a Veterinarian was on my agenda and even my parents laughed when I told them, "You're from Drumchapel" they would retort. My silent reply was always a courteous "Fuck You". Even though my school reports were good, always in the top 10 in my class of 40-50 kids my parents had no faith in their child. Probably a reflection of the troubling times they had to endure from my older brothers over their own individual problematic early years.

I had three older brothers, one sister both sides of me, one older and one younger. Their names are not important, they know who they are, you don't need to know! Being the youngest boy, I was constantly bullied and verbally abused by my elders. Never physically, well, almost never, but the torment was still, if not physically painful, even more effective emotionally, and caused me great anxiety in my early years.

They had the fun together, they had the train sets, the Scalextric, the Subbuteo. I was never allowed to play with them. I took my turn at all the joint family entertainment once they had bored and went off in their 'gang' to do something else. Sometimes I roped my younger sister into playing, which was good as I ensured I always won, by fair or foul means.

We were a relatively poor family in the wider scale of things but within the Drumchapel scale we were a rich family. Ours was one of the only families whose father had a car. A Morris 1000, split-screen, and all the accessories that would have made it worth a small fortune today if it had been kept pristine. My dad had to hand it back to his company every two years and get a new one. We were so rich that I had my own football. A real football, one without laces, a Mouldmaster that just about took your head off when you headed it. It was mine, my very own with no need to share and fight my brothers over it and I cherished it.

I spent hours with the only 'toy' I could call my own not knowing that the love for my football was leading me down a path in my life that would haunt me for five decades. I wasn't to know that then or I would have gladly given my ball to my brothers, been done with it, and be done with football, and concentrated on other 'goals' in my life. I didn't, I wish I had. I kept it and progressed to my fate at the hands of an individual who, fifty years later I can still see in my dreams, smell him, feel his touch, and am constantly reminded of the horrendous fear and confusion he implanted into the heart and mind of a young boy who only wanted to grow up with, and just be like other normal kids.

I was never really that good at football, to be honest. Always the sub, seldom the first-team choice whether that be for the School, Boys Brigade, Youth Teams, or a daily kick-about with my pals. I was never the last to be picked thankfully, nearly, but never the last. Not being the last picked meant I could play outfield as the last picked always had to be the goalie.

It was as a 12-year-old I began to rebel and forge my own identity, I wanted to be who I wanted to be rather than being one of the herd that by tradition, had to follow in their parents and their elder siblings' beliefs and values. Even when those same beliefs and values were wrong, misplaced, or morally corrupt you had to be a part of the herd. Not for me! I was the baby who rebelled to go on my own, the problem with that as many a 'Bambi' have found to their cost, leaving the herd leaves you in the path of Lions without the herd's protection. So, off I went into the unknown, a "Bambi" with only my own values as protection.

It was difficult to follow the families herd environment in any case. My Father was a sectarian bigot. R.I.P, but he was a nasty little man and there is no getting away from that. From an early age I was confused by his attitude and couldn't understand why he could hate people he did not even know? A staunch Rangers supporter, a season ticket holder at Ibrox for decades and never missed an away game as far as I can remember. My brothers followed his lead and hated all things Celtic, a mystery to me but maybe not being part of the herd kept me from following the same distasteful path in life.

Some aspects of our upbringing in Drumchapel as kids weren't acceptable to me. There were 4 boys in our family. We lived on Kinfauns Drive and within a stone's throw from us in Summerhill Drive were the Campbells. Four of them, all a similar age. The Campbells were Catholics, they went to the 'Catholic School', we went to the non-denomination School. There was constant war between the Woods family and the Campbells. 16-year-olds, 15-year-olds, 13 and 12-year-olds all fighting at every opportunity without any understandable reason. Why? Because it was the herd thing to do.

You didn't need to have a reason to dislike someone personally. You didn't need to have a reason to sucker-punch someone as you passed, you only needed to know what school they went to or which football colours the preferred for you to decide whether you hated them or not! I hated that rationale then and I still, to this day, hate it.

Now, I was left with a very difficult decision at a very young age. You see, my mum was a Roman Catholic, R.I.P. She never knew, I've never mentioned nor discussed it with her, but I discovered her hiding place years before and to this day have kept it a secret from the rest of my family. The only articles in her hiding place which was in the kitchen broom cupboard behind the electric meter were her Bible and Rosary Beads. Don't ask me how I discovered them, I was obviously searching for my own hiding place for something. What that was I cannot recall however as a pre-teen young boy; I have my suspicions. They obviously brought her some comfort as she dealt with the disgusting sectarian feelings and horrendous remarks directed at her from others within her own home. Even I, at such an early age, knew if my father found the Bible and Rosary Beads, he would have unceremoniously binned them and gave my mum hell, mentally and physically, for having them in a 'Protestant' household in the first place.

I can remember going to bed and crying for my mum sometimes after watching her sit in a room with football on the T.V. To hear her own husband and children referring to, 'catholic scum', 'fenian bastards', 'fucking the Pope' and many other anti-Catholic sentiments that I need not go into here. Most of you can imagine what they were anyway.

I used to turn and look at my mum when this was going on and saw tears in her eyes many times. To this day my mum's tears haunt me and to this day I have never forgiven my father nor my brothers for inflicting that on my mother. For what? The love of a fucking football team?

It was at that time probably, at 12 years old, that due to the disdain I had constructed for my father and brothers, not really my brother's fault I may add, their brainwashing had been effective and as being part of the herd, their remit was to follow the leader blindly, that I made a conscious decision not to be a part of it but to be Gordon Woods. A Gordon Woods who would go forward as he felt in his heart was the 'right thing to do'. Having that same 'right thing to do' attitude was to have a major impact on my life 50+ years down the line.

In the late '60s kids were totally unaware of

many of the things today's children must contend with. There were not even the 'stranger danger' campaigns we have introduced to our nation's children since. Social media did not exist, in fact neither did computers nor anything else that the kids of today take for granted. Many aspects of their introduction have been beneficial to the safety, security, and well-being of children of course making them much more aware and with a greater understanding of the dangers they can face from predators in their fragile lives. Predators who work alone, predators who work in groups and predators who tragically know how to remain invisible to everyone other than their poor child victims.

I met a young lad at the football field one Saturday morning. A lovely sunny day, unusual for Scotland to be fair, that's why I mentioned it. We both had our very own cherished footballs but mine was better. I had on my home-made Rangers top, and he wore his Celtic top. We were at different ends of the park as was the norm with the conflicting attire and ignored each other for some time. Eventually I thought why were we doing this, two young lads 100 yards apart because of our families misplaced beliefs that this was the way to do things? I made the first move and kicked my precious Mouldmaster in his direction. He kindly kicked it back returning it to me. I kicked it over to him again and he returned it to me on the volley... *Impressive.*

This continued for a few minutes before we realised, we were no longer 100 yards apart but more like 50, then 30, then 10, we were now within earshot of course and started a conversation. Within an hour we were mates and played together for a few hours with no concerns for the tops we were displaying. His name was 'Keith' (for now), and we met up on many occasions after that. Two individuals from either side of the divide who were playing, enjoying life, and friendship together, and without the stench that had enveloped our respective families for years.

One thing I did notice about Keith very early on in our now solid friendship was the fact he did not indeed have a Celtic Football Club top on at all...

His Hoops wore the badge of the Celtic Boys' Club!

I never questioned him on that for some time. I wish I hadn't, but I did and that started me on the road to a lifetime of regret. Keith spoke highly of the Celtic Boys Club. He told me his 'Coach' Jim Torbett was a good friend as well as a 'coach'. Jim Torbett would always have time to listen to the problems he was having in his own little inexperienced life and offer solutions to ease any or all the concerns his fragile mind was battling. He offered to introduce me to Jim Torbett, and I declined. One Catholic friend was enough to contend with at this point in time. Although I felt I was supporting my mum I had begun to feel guilty about what this would do to my father and brothers, should the truth ever get out about my new associate. Guilt? Yes, not the same guilt the predators use, the guilt a family uses.

I absolutely recall getting ready one Saturday morning to go out with the intention of meeting Keith at the football pitch. My mother asked me where I was going, and I told her to meet Keith for a kick-about. She asked me if he was a school friend as I hadn't mentioned the name before. I took the opportunity to confide in my mum at that point. "Keith goes to St Pius School mum, he's a Celtic supporter and a Catholic". Her raised eyebrow invited me to continue. "Mum, we are good pals and just play football together, he plays for Celtic Boys Club and is a great player. He teaches me a lot". I awaited a bollocking, to be honest having the belief she would chastise me for being so stupid in consideration of how my father and brothers would react. She smiled and simply said "I'm so proud of you Gordon, I love you, let's keep it just between the two of us for now, go and enjoy yourself".

Now whether or not that was the one and only time my mother was actually proud of me I'll never know now but one thing for sure, it would have been the most important. It endorsed everything that I was beginning to believe in, rubber-stamped my earlier decisions, and gave me some pride that I had so far been lacking in myself as I went forward.

I had put sectarianism, racism, and any other isms to the back of my mind and was confident I would never allow them to surface again. Homophobia didn't come into it, I was unaware of it in those days, I had no knowledge that same-sex relationships were actually a 'thing'. I was totally naïve to all of that and to the dangers that lurked in all the dark places I had yet to experience. The Sexual Offences act of 1967 had yet to be brought into Law so that had no bearing on any of my beliefs or the stance that I was taking in life.

Keith and I continued to meet and on occasion would discuss the differing views our respective families held. We were in agreement that it was not the way to be going forward and pledged to support each other regardless of the commotion our friendship may or may not cause at our respective home. He did however reside within 50 yards of the Campbells, so I had to be careful going backward and forwards on visits.

I had made the first step to being the person I wanted to be, a young individual, beginning too correctly mature, humanely, and respectfully.

During one kick about Keith invited me to Celtic

Park for a Saturday game. They were playing Partick Thistle. He had been given two complimentary stand tickets and I excitedly accepted his invitation. I had only been to one other professional match and that was when my father had taken me to Ibrox. Rangers played Falkirk and won 6-0. My Father I recall gave me a slap on the ear for not celebrating the 6th goal properly! I was so excited about going with Keith to the Celtic match, albeit secretly. Celtic won the game with a handful of goals, and nobody gave me a slap.

On the bus home Keith asked me if I wanted to come with him on the Thursday evening to Celtic Park as they had trials at Barrowfield for the Celtic Boys' Club, and he had been asked to bring anyone along who he deemed good enough to be signed. I was doubtful, this would have been an eruption of massive proportions if by some strange quirk of fate, I was to have been accepted into the 'Celtic Family'. The fall out would have been heard throughout Drumchapel, my family (other than my mother) would probably disown me, and I would be on my own, an outcast, an unloved family member and labelled for life as a traitor and a 'fenian bastard' probably. Then I summarised and realised it wouldn't be that much different from what I was already experiencing in family life.

Keith was very persuasive though. He knew the problems I was having at home; he knew I was saddened by it all and needed direction. He really believed I had a chance and convinced me as the bus turned into Kinfauns Drive. I agreed to accompany him and take my chances, I wish upon all wishes I had not!

As we went our separate ways that day, he winked at me and told me I'd be fine and not to worry about going on the Thursday to the trials. He was so wrong!

My Celtic dream, that would morph into a nightmare, a nightmare that no child should be forced into, had begun.

2. AN OPPORTUNITY ARISES - TRIALS.....

Keith and I met up around 4.30 p.m. on Thursday and headed into town. I had told my mother I was going to football training at the B.B. (Boys Brigade) and she believed me, I think. I'm sure she was fully aware that something wasn't quite right but kept it to herself. She didn't ask as her previous experience with her children had taught her that she would most definitely be lied to in any case. I realised once I had boarded the bus with Keith later that not having taken my 'Mouldmaster' with me was a sure-fire indication that everything was not as it seemed. I felt a terrible guilt lying to her after she had been so understanding about Keith earlier but really, I felt the less she knew, the less my father would have to throw in her face as he had done so many times before, achieving nothing!

It was quite a surreal journey. I was very quiet, and Keith wouldn't shut up. He told me over and over again what to expect and at no time did I hear a single word. I was excited, overly, attempting to mentally prepare myself for what lay ahead. Of course, if I had had any inkling of what lay ahead, in the long run, I would have escaped, I would have run faster than I had ever run before, with or without a cherished ball at my feet.

The journey took us just over an hour. It entailed a bus from Drumchapel into the city centre then a short subway ride to Argyle Street where we caught the number 64 to Auchenshuggle (I kid you not!) and embarked once we caught sight of the stadium.

Keith knew the way of course as he had often made the journey but for me it was a new adventure and one that I am sure not many 13-year-olds hadn't dreamt about.

As we started to walk towards the stadium the enormity of it all started to take its toll and I felt an overwhelming feeling of dread. I can't in all honesty explain it. All I knew was, something was telling me to give up long before I had even kicked a ball that night.

Keith and I walked up through the car park past the old school that was on London Road. The school was on our right. The view in front of us was that of Celtic Football Club Stadium. I remember thinking that within those walls were the European Cup, and four other domestic trophies Celtic had won the previous season. I still found it unreasonable, and most certainly unthinkable a few months beforehand that I was soon to be a part of that history, that year, without doubt, Celtic Football Club's greatest ever year. Even as a probable failed trialist I could still say I had been there. As we passed the end of the school walls we turned to the right and approached a small building with the entrance door on the side. Although I felt a tinge of disappointment that the main doors of the stadium were not where we were heading, I accepted that this was as good as I could expect with the boys' club and my thoughts started to turn positive.

Now there has been a lot of controversy as to where the Celtic Boys' Club met in those early days. Many people have been quite strongly vocal, in their opinion that the building I remember going into was never used for the Celtic Boys' Club and was in fact the Celtic pools office, the ticket office, etc but never used for Celtic Boys' Club. I cannot speak for subsequent years when its use may have changed but I am, without any doubt, confident that this was the building we used to change before we ran up London Road in our football kit to Barrowfield training ground and returned there after training to change again for home. This has also been confirmed by others who played at that time.

We trained there indoors a couple of times when the weather was so bad that going to Barrowfield was not an option, or when the Barrowfield grass was undergoing maintenance for players far more important than us. Generally, though the building was only used by Celtic Boys' Club as a changing facility. Of course, there were times after the training when the children would require a sports massage to account for any strains or injuries, they had picked up at Barrowfield! There was an area within the building to accommodate this. The building has since been demolished; I believe around 2016 when Celtic Park was partially rebuilt. A move I am sure helped many young lads put distressing memories away to hopefully never resurface.

As Keith and I entered the building, again, the enormity of everything slapped the breath out of me. My first vision was of 20-30 young lads all preparing for their training/trial in Celtic kit. Celtic Football Club official strips, the official strips of the European Cup Winners, why was I even there? Keith took me to a space where we could get changed and I started to get my own kit from my bag. Not my home-made Rangers top I hasten to add, I had thought that one out already, I had taken an old school strip I had worn from the previous season.

The formality was certainly impressive. All the boys were in the Celtic kit, not just the shirts but also the shorts, socks, shin pads etc, all the official Celtic stuff. The Boys' Club officials were all smartly dressed in their crisp white shirts accompanied by official Celtic Boys' Club green blazers and ties, both bearing the Celtic Boys' Club badge, grey trousers, and shiny black shoes. You had to look very carefully at first to notice that the Boys Club Badge was of a slightly different (only slightly) design from the official one that was indeed copywritten by Celtic Football Club. The badges have changed over the years, and I believe this was the first one before the Celtic Boys' Club name was changed in 2018 after a sizeable payment from Celtic to finance their re-branding. Celtic wanted rid of the elephant in the room. It appeared, far too late, the Club wanted to distance themselves from the Boys' Club and its horrific history. It had no right to think this was even a possibility, its involvement would haunt them in years to come.

I removed my jacket and shirt, and as I was preparing to put on my own football top an official of the Boys Club appeared and handed me a Celtic strip to wear and a yellow bib. The bib indicated I was a trialist. My heart skipped a little, I really was about to wear the Hoops of Glasgow Celtic, I was to become a Celtic Lion, maybe not for long but for the rest of my life I could I say I officially wore the hoops. I thanked him.

He introduced himself and gave his name as Jim Torbett and he progressed to let me know that I had been expected, Keith had told him all about me. I wasn't sure if that was a good or a bad thing, turned out to be a bad thing, a very bad thing.

As a group we made our own way up London Road to Barrowfield. No team bus, no coach, no cars, just our own little legs running up the London Road with the occasional car tooting either in support or disgust. We never looked back to determine which. It took all of probably 5 minutes from memory and we went through the gates, past the team's changing facility and onto the very same grass that the Lisbon Lions had prepared to meet Inter Milan in the Estadio National in Lisbon in May 1967 to fight like gladiators for the coveted European Cup.

I can remember doing a lot of running backward and forwards, speed trials, corner kicks, and shots at goal. I was always an inside-right (as they were called in those days) and wore the number 8 shirt. The coach told me to move to inside left and that left me, well and truly, in the proverbial shit. I couldn't kick a ball with my left foot to save my life, so I constantly had to turn to get the ball onto my right. That obviously highlighted a massive problem for the dream makers.

We formed two groups, trialists against the current Celtic Boys and I am quite sure we got hammered, but in fairness the ref had a Celtic Boys' Club blazer on. Take from that what you will. One thing I can remember was the overwhelming pride I felt at being there, wearing the hoops officially, and the occasion as a whole.

Anything else that happened at the training ground that night escapes me. I do remember running back to the changing facility, the controversial one, along London Road. We were still being attacked by car horns albeit different ones, to change back into our own gear and await our fate.

As we entered the changing rooms the bib wearing newbies were taken to one side immediately. There was to be no allowances made for the dreams of the children who had staked their future success on a few hours of observation. There was to be no gentle let down or any understanding of how a crushed dream can affect the mental stability of a child who had given their all, but still just not good enough to convince those with the responsibility of selection who sentenced the boys without showing any emotional respect. They were either left ecstatic at having passed the grade or left lonely and distressed at being failures. I cannot recall any parents being there so I can only assume these failures had to find their own way home to announce their non-success to their respective families. I felt I knew how they were feeling though I was in the fortunate position where I had no-one to tell or admit my failing to.

Keith watched on eagerly, awaiting my own result with great interest. A blazer sauntered over and pointed to one of the lads, "You have been unsuccessful" he announced, "You have been selected" to another and progressed down the line pointing to a young dreamer in turn cruelly informing them of their fate. He was very particular in announcing his heart-breaking, to some, decision to avoid any doubt. My turn came... "You have been unsuccessful".

I turned and went over to my place to change for the long journey home and to be consoled by Keith. I don't think I felt that bad to be honest as I had expected it really and throughout the process had felt massively out of my depth.

Keith seemed more upset than me. A good mate, but there was nothing he could do to change the decision that had been made. He made things a little brighter when he announced that Jim Torbett had agreed to drive us back to Drumchapel rather than go by public transport. I had no idea why but was quite happy to accept. Apparently, it was a common occurrence for Keith to be driven home.

Initial talk in the car was about the Celtic Football Club players and members of the Celtic management team that had been noticed watching the boys at the trials. I hadn't seen them. Not that I would have recognised them anyway, but it was evident they were big names and that fact had made a huge impression on Keith and Torbett. I was unimpressed and did not care.

I sat in the back and Keith sat in the front passenger seat beside Torbett who was driving of course. I remained quiet and left the two of them to chatter on about other things that had occurred that night. I cannot remember any of their additional conversation, primarily because I wasn't really listening. As we arrived in Kinfauns Drive, Keith and I prepared to get out of the car together at Keith's' house. I only had a walk of 100 yards or so to my own home.

Torbett got out the car and he turned to me, he put his hand onto my shoulder, squeezed it before saying, "Just ignore that Gordon, I'll speak to him, and you just make sure you're at training next week". It is easy to make statements in hindsight, but I can, in all honesty, even at that early stage, confirm that his action made me feel, at the very least, uncomfortable, very uncomfortable. I knew not why, I just did!

I had been given a reprieve by Torbett. For some reason, he had seen something in me that he liked. Was it my amazing footballing skills, did he see a sparkling new future for me, perhaps he had a new discovery to announce to the world?

No, it was none of those I must admit. It transpired in the months to come it certainly wasn't my abilities on the field of play. I was caught in a filthy paedophiles trap, a target, a Torbett target, a target before I had even kicked a ball in earnest for Celtic.

As my story unfolds it will become clear that

certain events of my journey 50 years ago are still strong in my memory bank. I can recall many things in meticulous detail regardless of the importance they attach themselves to my journey. Small things, that may be of little importance on their own but massively important in the overall story are as clear as if they happened yesterday. As I progress there will be times when I just have to say, "I can't remember". There are many areas I am unclear on. Perhaps areas that are of much more relevance to what I was about to endure. I cannot, in all honesty, put these ever-growing grey areas to paper unless I am 100% sure and I am confident that what I am writing is factual. Without that confidence they will have to remain a secret between me and my subconscious... And my own unjustified guilt.

Does this sound like a 'separate entity'?

The building (ringed) where we changed prior to heading for Barrowfield in 1967, within Celtic's grounds. The building has now been demolished.

3. FAILURE AVOIDED

I walked from the drop-off point to my home elated. After the initial disappointment, Torbett getting involved and over-riding the previous decision that had been made, ensured I had avoided failure and was now indeed about to be welcomed into 'The Celtic Family'. It was a bizarre opportunity that I had no desire to disbelieve, and I certainly was not going to question it. I had assumed Torbett was happy with my performance and had saw a future in my ability that others had not. He was the main man at Celtic Boys' Club, and I was proud to think he had confidence in me as I had total confidence in him. Torbett was going to turn me into a real footballer, a star, a hero, a Celtic Football Club hero.

When it eventually struck home that I had been successful at the trials I realised I had the enormous mountain to climb to break the very sad news to my father and my brothers. On arriving home, I went immediately to my room. I shared a large room with my three brothers, and I slept in a bottom bunk bed. The two youngest had the bottom bunks with the two eldest reserving the top. I think at the time that rule was accepted in many families and to attempt to rebel was not in your best interests. I had the room to myself as it was still fairly early and I wanted to be asleep before my brothers arrived, one by one, at their specified time to retire for the night. My mum came into the room to ask if I was OK as I hadn't acknowledged anyone on my trip from the front door to my room. I assured her everything was good and that I was just tired after the BB training. She accepted that and slipped out of the room leaving me in the dark.

I buried my face into my pillow, and I cried, I wept, I was bordering sobbing. Why? I don't know! Maybe I was just so happy at my success, maybe I was just so unhappy that I had again felt the need to lie to my mother, maybe I was just fearful of my emerging mountain or maybe, just maybe, there was a ticking time bomb of apprehension in my immature head.

I awoke early and headed downstairs already dressed for school, the non-denomination school, and mum was already in the kitchen after seeing my father off to his work. Cornflakes were prepared for my breakfast (as always) and I was aware of my mother's eyes concentrating on me, flitting back and forth to other things intermittently but eventually returning to me to rest. I felt uncomfortable but not threatened in any way. I avoided her eye without realising my avoidance of her gaze was as sure a sign of my guilt to her as any other.

Eventually I had to admit defeat and I caught her eye just as her face broke into a smile. My mum was Irish, from County Cork, her Irish eyes smiled, as they were supposed to, and she had a smile that left even the most fearful feeling secure. "You're up to something?" were the words that broke the silence. "We need to have a talk when you're home from school". It wasn't a question but a demand. I smiled back and asked her why she thought I was up to something. She immediately threw down on the table in front of me the used tickets for the Glasgow subway and for the number 64 bus to Auchenshuggle! "Playing for the BB, my arse", is all she said. I should have known she would go through my pockets. I had been aware of this intrusion into my privacy many times before although after what I had put her through at times, I had always justified it to myself and never thought bad of her for doing so. My smile proved her point, and I was left with no option other than to agree to our chat after school.

It was difficult keeping my new information to myself. I was keen whilst at school that day to announce the news to my mates of my acceptance into The Celtic Family but didn't want it to get back to my brothers at this early stage. I felt it better to speak to my mum first and it was important to do everything I could to avoid being murdered by my brothers before we had a chance to talk. I saw two of my three brothers during the course of the day, the eldest had left by this point after completing his allocated time with no qualifications, but I said nothing, neither did they.

At 4 p.m. on the final bell of the day I left the school gates, crossed the road, and walked through our front door. All within 20 seconds. Mum was waiting for me of course and indicated that we would wait until my siblings had appeared, had their preferred snack, and then disappeared to do their own thing without a care in the world... yet!

My confession began with an apology. My guilt at my deception was at this moment staggeringly paramount. Much more important than my new career as a professional footballer for the current European Champions. I was fully aware, and immensely fearful, of the shock this news was about to be released on the Woods family. Not just within our own household. I had a grandfather, a string of uncles, cousins, and family friends who would all be mounting their claim to comment on my treason in due course. Added to those would be the reaction of my own mates at school, my non-denomination school, my Protestant mates. My one and only Catholic mate would stand by me, but I doubted that would be sufficient for me to take a stand and 'do the right thing'.

It was all, perhaps, to become too much for a 13-year-olds ability to cope with its magnitude. I had midway through our chat already began to determine that this scenario was just not worth it. Certainly not worth the effect it would have on the relationship between my mother and her immediate family. She did not deserve the abuse that would inevitably be thrust into her face from their herded, pathetic beliefs. This was in the 60's and today in the 2020's nothing has changed, a sad fact I can do nothing about!

I started by explaining the original invitation from Keith. I confided in mum how that had made me feel valued, a new experience for me unfortunately. I went on to hopefully make her grasp that in my own child's eyes this was not an action that was processed to interfere, condone nor criticise either side of the divide. It was the only offer that had come my way and despite who the organisation was making that offer it was important to me to see it through. Mum listened acutely, perhaps for the first time in my early years my opinions were important enough to garnish attention. It was easy to see my mother relaxing as I progressed, she was beginning to understand and accepted my reasons for the secrecy. She didn't blame me, it was what she would have expected from any of her children, it just happened to be her youngest son.

Her pride was obvious once I gave her the news that I had been accepted, albeit with the interference of Torbett. I didn't mention that part. I explained that I was now expected to attend The Celtic Boys' Club training every Thursday and that I would be expected to wear, I presumed, the official uniform. Blazer, tie, grey trousers, and shiny black shoes.

When all the explaining was over and done with it was my mother's turn to give her verdict. I honestly did not know what to expect. I was awaiting, I think, her dismissing the whole idea as impossible in consideration of the circumstances. She left the table and went upstairs leaving me alone in the kitchen to gather my thoughts and reflect on the preceding 30 minutes or so. I began to convince myself she would never condone anything that involved any involvement with Celtic Football Club, I would probably have to give up on any thoughts of scoring the cup winner at Hampden wearing the hoops, on their behalf.

Mum returned and her only concern seemed to be how I was feeling. Once I confided in her what my thoughts were now, she shook her head and took my hand into hers. "Go for it, Gordon, it's important to follow your dreams and as long as no-one gets innocently hurt, then it's worth it". I brought it to her attention that my dad would be hurt, and her reply was "Not innocently".

Mum and I hatched our plan, she would talk to my dad and explain everything to him. My brothers would be commanded to back me in my adventure and give me all the support I needed. Although I was very doubtful of this, stranger things have happened, especially in the world of football.

I did say earlier that some memories of my journey are there to recall and put onto these pages for your attention. Others are not. I cannot for the life of me remember what happened next within the context of the anticipated fall-out at the family home. My next memory is of being initially ridiculed by my dad when I arrived home with my Celtic Boys Club blazer and tie in a Galbraiths Stores (grocery shop) paper bag all carefully folded and placed in my new Celtic Boys' Club hold-all. I went to my room and put them on with my crisp white shirt from school. I had the shiny black shoes but not the grey trousers, so I settled for black.

My dad sat in the chair that we were not allowed to occupy in the lounge as I came into the room. He said I looked smart and proceeded to take a Polaroid snap. Nothing else was said. No degree of support was offered but in fairness neither were there any detrimental comments made so that was something to be thankful for. Neither can I recall the initial reaction of my brothers. The fact that I cannot, would probably point to their reaction being supportive rather than the contrary.

So, it would appear things were not as bad as had been expected.

To be honest a bit of a disappointment and an

extreme anti-climax. I fear, in reality, I was secretly, sadly, looking forward to the expected confrontation and for my opportunity to tell them what I really thought of them, their behaviour towards our mum and how their vile thought processes were despicable.

That was put on hold, for now!

Does this sound like a 'separate entity'?

4. GROOMING BEGINS

The 'pied piper' of Celtic Boys' Club told young players he could make their dreams come true but there was a price to pay. I truly believe that many boys were taken into the Boys' Club purely for the purpose of being abused. These victims lacked the skill level, right from the very start, that Celtic were looking for, they were never going to make the grade demanded by professional clubs to progress in football. Those that did make the grade or had a distinct footballing promise were left alone, they were deemed out of bounds by the paedophiles as they had to ensure a steady supply of young blood could be delivered to Celtic Football Club to ensure the Celtic Boys' Club's continuance. Even then, sometimes, the animals crossed the line.

Where did Keith go? That was a question I posed to myself very early on in my time with The Celtic Family. Keith and I had travelled to training together every Thursday for quite a while. We met up at the bus stop just outside his block of flats on the corner of Kinfauns Drive and Summerhill Road. Torbett would always drive myself and Keith home after training. One night he wasn't there. I didn't have time to wait so I travelled into Celtic Park on my own. I honestly cannot recall anything more about Keith. I will say he did re-appear over 50 years later during a High Court trial. I would love to get some answers to my many questions that evolved as my time with the Celtic Family progressed.

Where did Stein's son go? Jock Stein's son, George also played for the boys' club in '67/'68. He was another who suddenly disappeared with no communication or explanation given to any of the boys officially. His sudden, quite obvious non-attendance was very much a talking point between all the boys. I remember asking Torbett on the way home one evening and was given an 'unofficial' explanation. Not that I believe it for one second due to it coming from the mouth of Torbett, but I will record what he said.

That 'unofficial' explanation from Torbett was as follows... All the boys were ordered to attend for several nights to conduct a fund-raising by doing a house-to-house collection. I was given the area of Hillhead in Glasgow. We dropped off small brown envelopes through the letterboxes of 100+ or so letterboxes the first night. The envelopes had requested a donation and that they would be collected the following night. From memory I think it was for something like 'The Glasgow Association of Boys' Clubs' but I can't be sure. We then retraced our steps the following evening knocking on the doors and collecting the envelopes. These were all taken back to the changing facility outside Celtic Park, opened and the money counted by the officials. My own envelopes, as did all the other boys, contained a healthy mixture of coppers, the occasional sixpence and from the very wealthy a shilling, a florin and in exceptional cases a half-crown. However, when the count was made from

Stein's son every envelope had a copper or two and they appeared to have been opened and resealed. George was never seen at the boys' club again. This explanation I must re-iterate came from the mouth of Torbett, perhaps the truth, perhaps manufactured to hide something far more distasteful? I cannot say.

Throughout the time I was there several other young lads had also suddenly stopped attending the training sessions. We never found out why nor was it ever brought up in training or team meetings. It seemed to everyone very strange that potentially highly gifted footballers with their dreams could walk away from this amazing opportunity that had been presented to them but that's exactly what they did.

Torbett now drove me home after training each night. I was unaware at that time where he lived though it became evident later that he had in fact been passing his home in Pinkston Drive to drive an extra 30 minutes each way to take me 'safely' home. The regular journey took just under an hour. Torbett used that time to discuss with me the issues I was having at the club and was very supportive in any problems I was experiencing. They worried me far less knowing I had the main man watching my back, and ensuring I was comfortable at the club during my early days. His concerns, the conversations, the advice, about my welfare was generally more concentrated however in relation to my problems at home. He was very understanding and quickly gained my confidence to open up to him. I sought his advice and he always seemed to have the answers to make me feel more secure. Torbett claimed my trust and he became the one person who I knew I could trust with my innermost thoughts. He became my friend as he was once Keith's friend. I believed in him implicitly, and opened up to him often and that trust was twisted and used in the most sinister way.

The first-time things started to go wrong was when I had had a particularly bad week at home. I had witnessed my father physically attack my mother and had intervened. At 13 years old I had grabbed my father by the throat and pinned him to a wall demanding he cease, or I would rip his fucking head off. He raised a fist to strike, thought better of it, lowered it, pushed me away, he left the room. Mum and I were of course in a bad way for a long time, and I had confided this to Torbett the next training night.

After training we left the changing facility to go home in Torbett's car. We discussed what had happened that week at home during the journey. As we approached my house in Kinfauns Drive, Torbett pulled over with 100 or so yards to go, parking beside the long row of bushes and trees. He said it would be better not to go home yet as I seemed to be upset at the events and it would be better to talk for a while and get it all off my chest. We talked for a half hour or so and I was feeling much better.

I told him I was OK to go home now, and he said he needed the toilet and went into the bushes to do the necessary. When he returned to the car it was obvious, he had not buttoned himself up and proceeded to perform a sexual act on himself. He put his left hand down inside my trousers and progressed to touch me intimately. I absolutely froze and was in a state of shock, amid the fear. My mind was racing, and I couldn't quite accept the situation and certainly had no idea what to do to make it stop.

My father always parked his car underneath a streetlight opposite our home for safety reasons. I fixed my stare onto his car and then the light, not daring to divert my gaze anywhere else. I was hoping my dad would come out for something from his car, see us and make it stop. He didn't. He never did.

Torbett did what he had wanted and afterwards acted as he had been acting before the attack. It didn't seem to be anything unusual for him and that confused me terribly. Without mentioning anything that had just taken place he asked if I was OK, and I replied that I was. What else was I to say? I was in a panic by that stage and wanted to be sick.

My house (centre) and X marks where abuse took place many times.

Once he had tidied himself, he leant over and opened the passenger door of the car. I got a hold of my kitbag and started to leave when he took a grip of my thigh. "I won't tell your mum and dad what you've done. If they knew they would be so angry and stop, you coming to the Boys' Club so it's better we keep it to ourselves. You don't want to leave all your pals at the Club do you"? I shook my head and as I left, he reiterated "I promise Gordon, I won't tell them".

As I walked the short distance home, I started to get upset but I was well aware of the implications if my parents were to see my distress. I composed myself by sitting at my front door for what seemed like an eternity. I eventually entered the house saying nothing to anyone other than I was tired and was going to my bed.

As I lay in my bed, I started to go over everything that had happened but was at a total loss to make sense of anything. I felt nauseous and went to the bathroom, but I was unable to vomit. I wanted it all to be yesterday so I could relive it all and not do what I had just done. I had put Torbett into a position whereupon he could get into trouble. I could be forced out of the Boys' Club and my footballing future was in serious jeopardy all because of my stupid actions. I was so angry with myself; I had been so brainless and vowed it would never happen again. I lay awake for most of the night going over things again and again but every time it had the same conclusion. I was so ashamed of myself.

Despite my vow, it did happen again. Many times, and each time I continued to fix my gaze onto the streetlight above my dad's car. It faded and became much brighter before it faded again. It did that many times before I was eventually freed and was allowed to go home to my unsuspecting parents. Each time my guilt manifested many times over and I was horrified I was putting my friend, my hero, and career builder into this seriously awkward position.

The Saturday after it had happened the first time was game free though Torbett still telephoned the house and told me to meet him in Dinos Italian Restaurant in Sauchiehall Street at 2p.m. Once I arrived, he ordered lunch and he wanted to talk about what had happened. He was concerned if I had said anything to anyone and he re-iterated the consequences should anyone find out. He told me I was improving so well with my training, and it would be a shame to let all that hard work go to waste.

We were taken to Dinos regularly after training. Sometimes a few of the lads at a time and often just myself with Torbett. Since the initial incident of abuse Torbett became much more tactile with me at every opportunity. In the car, the restaurant, even at training when we were alone, he would have his arm round me, touching me inappropriately. He often took my hand, and he would rest his hand on my thigh and stroke me like his puppy. Although it made me feel very uncomfortable there was no apparent way to make it stop without me losing everything. I was prepared to accept it as I hadn't previously considered having to pay for my chance of fame. The price of stardom was previously unknown to me, I assumed this was the price everyone paid. Looking back now it is obvious Torbett was making the constant touching and the closeness the norm, preparing me into acceptance of the horrors that was to come, when they came.

Torbett had bought my silence with the threat of a bulldozed career, and it was all my fault. He made that very clear. I never thought for one second that the blame was not mine.

One very clear memory of the effect of this was that for the first time in my life, at 14-years-old, I started to drink alcohol and smoke cigarettes. At the end of Kinfauns Drive there was an off-licence, it was actually on Spey Road. I would go often and ask someone, anyone, who was old enough and going into the shop to buy me a bottle of "Old English White Wine". There was never any shortage of amused, obliging young men. I still remember it cost fourteen shillings. A packet of cigarettes and matches I think two or three shillings so I would give them a pound, and they could keep the change.

I would take my carry-out into the Bluebell Woods behind Summerhill Road, always on my own, and stay there until I was drunk but still capable of getting home. Well, that was the plan though many times I would wake up in the middle of the night, in the woods, cold and damp and drunk. Always fearful of the abuse I was going to take from my parents when I got home. Many a night I was able to sneak into the unlocked back door and into my bed without them being aware of me being plastered and stinking of Woodbines.

Strange things would manifest into the mind of a young boy. Just prior to my abuse starting the news was full of Hyndley and Brady, the Moors murderers who abducted, abused, and murdered children in England. Can you imagine the fear that would conjure up in the mind of a child terrified that they could well be travelling a similar path to those poor children?

Thankfully Torbett was very understanding and never told anyone thus allowing my career to stay on track. He was a very good friend indeed. I knew Torbett would ensure my well-being and he would look after me. I had every confidence in him, and I would have done anything to make him proud of me. One day I would play at Parkhead for Jim Torbett.

5. THE CELTIC FAMILY

Despite what had begun to take place my sights were still firmly focussed on one day playing in a European Cup Final with the Hoops and number 8 on my back. Torbett continued to praise me on my commitment to the training and was very convincing that my day would be very soon upon us, and I would be given my time to convince the Celtic officials of my undoubted worth.

The training sessions were always a great event with the Celtic manager Jock Stein and other Directors/Officials occasionally in attendance, together with a handful of the players showing on interest in their cheeky young challengers. We were all aware that we were being studied, and each evening of action would bring either praise or censure. The boys all worked hard and regardless of their individual skill would give their all. No cup was up for grabs, no title at stake, no medals to be won but the effort was always monumental and an indication of the massive dreams operating those little feet. We were all so proud to be a junior member of the Celtic family. Membership was continually demonstrated by the dedication of the Celtic officials in attendance amongst other things. On one particular night, I was messing around and misbehaving with one of the other lads. As the whistle blew to return to the changing rooms Stein called me and the other lad's name after he had seen us larking about, he demanded we do another 3 laps of the park before we could make our way down London Road. His eyes were everywhere, and he never missed an opportunity to set you in the right direction.

At absolutely no time, never, were there any indications, either verbal or non-verbal that we were an organisation not linked to Celtic Football Club itself. If indeed, as has been stated recently, we were a separate organisation, then the Celtic Football Club officials and the Boys' Club officials were liars, cheats, and vultures, preying on the aspirations of children and making them believe the opposite to be true. They went out of their way, persistently, to ensure the boys were convincingly aware of their family membership. Tickets for games, tours of the stadium, often mixing with many players and officials, training at Barrowfield, wearing the official Celtic kit, and gaining the respect of every other Boys' Club football team we played against with them being led to believe we were indeed Celtic's Boys' Club. Remember this was what I experienced in 1967, it continued until the late 90's and possible even until the 2020's.

We were welcomed into Celtic Park itself many times to watch the team train and were fit enough to clean their boots, literally, on quite a few occasions. Visits to the Trophy Room were commonplace, walking the corridors of Celtic

Park was a privilege often afforded to the boys, though only when accompanied by a Celtic or a Boys' Club official.

One evening event I had attended, when the Celtic officials and players were in attendance, I had the need to go the bathroom. As I returned to the room Stein approached me in the corridor on his way, I presumed, to do the same. There was a brief conversation. "How are you enjoying yourself with the Boys' Club?" I lied and told him I was enjoying it. "Do you think you're going to make it with Celtic?" he asked. "That's up to you Mr. Stein." I respectfully replied. "Yes, it is up to me son, good luck!" That simple exchange told me, and tells me to this day, Jock Stein saw the Celtic Boys' Club as Celtics, playing under their banner and representing them in every single match we played. That was why discipline was so important and the constant reminders from officials to behave at all times because we were representing Celtic Football Club, Champions of Europe.

We were allocated stand tickets for the Celtic home games most of which I would give out to others as I always attended the matched with Torbett. During these matches, it was quite common for me to be in the company of many of the Club's greatest ambassadors at half and full time in the hospitality rooms. Never a Hoop in site but an abundance of blazers, ties, crisp white shirts, and well-polished shoes.

What was strangely accepted though was the fact that I would accompany Torbett to matches at Parkhead often. I was also with Torbett many times in a non-Boys' Club setting. Official engagements at Celtic Park which would involve the Celtic Football Club's first-team players and management. I was always with Torbett in his car as we left the training sessions. Why was none of that ever questioned? Why was it apparently deemed normal for Torbett to have the same young boy with him everywhere he went? I could understand it if there was perhaps a different boy each time as that could have been seen as giving the proud youngsters a chance to experience and be a part of the Celtic Family in turn. But for well over a year, it was me and only me. Red warning flags were not hoisted I can assume because the abnormality of it was normal, and acceptable for Torbett.

Does this sound like a 'separate entity'?

6. THE ABUSE

The constant touching and sick preparation for what was in store continued virtually each and every night that Torbett drove me home. The streetlight became my best friend in place of my filthy abuser and after a while, I and my body got used to the intrusion that I hated. On one occasion I remember him asking me if I was OK with a grin on his face that truly frightened me. I was in tears and that had prompted him asking, he didn't always ask. Most times he would do what he wanted and end the night as if nothing had happened. I told him I wasn't comfortable with what he was doing and that I really wanted him to stop. Once I even made up a story about a new girlfriend who I really liked and didn't want to upset her by doing these things with him. This seemed to amuse him, and I remember him asking me, as he laughed, if she could get me a game and a career playing for Celtic!

It was the same night that a very sinister comment was made that that changed my thoughts completely and installed a new level of fear within me. The conversation started after Torbett had had his entertainment and he asked if I would like to take our friendship a stage further. I truly had no idea what he meant and said so. He told me he had a lot of work to do at home preparing medals for the Boys' Club Awards and that he needed me to help. It would be easier, apparently, if I stayed overnight at his home. He said other boys would be there and we would also be paying a friendly game and that I would play. We could have an evening together having a bit of fun as we helped him. When I told him I couldn't do that because my parents wouldn't allow it, he told me to tell them I was going to play in a match in England and that I'd be away overnight. I still said I couldn't and froze at what he said next. "You'll be OK Gordon, you know I don't ever hurt you, we just have a bit of fun together, it's normal and you know I would never hurt you, don't you"? No Mr Torbett, I didn't!

My young mind tried to calculate, tried to understand what he had just said and, why it was said. I came to a quick conclusion that, despite the fact he had never actually physically hurt me at that point, he was saying if I didn't comply then he would. Perhaps that meant he would physically hurt me or alternatively was threatening to tell my parents everything.

I agreed to speak to my parents about our 'Away Match' and he told me to arrange it for the Saturday that was now just 9 days away.

That brought a whole new understanding, or so I thought, into the degradation. Here was I, most definitely being blackmailed, and forced into accepting and allowing his abuse to continue. Failure to comply would bring a whole new world of pain to me, either physically or mentally with my parents being told. I could not imagine the distress I would be subjected to at home should my father and brothers find out I had behaved in this way. The fear of both just confirmed to me that the status quo should be upheld, and I had no option other than to continue along this depressing route, rather than my parents getting involved.

Mum had agreed for me to go on the 'trip' and said she would discuss it with my father. I took my overnight bag and met up with Torbett at Dinos Restaurant. When I arrived, there was another of the boys sitting opposite Torbett on the bench seating and I took my place beside Torbett. Obviously, I am not in the position to name the youngster as I have been unable to make contact with him for his permission to do so (I haven't even tried to be honest as it's unfair on him). For now, we'll call him Billy.

We ate and had a drink before heading out and we were on our way to the high-rise flats in Pinkston Drive within the hour. It became quickly obvious that there was no game taking place, that was a big disappointment as I hadn't had many opportunities to play prior to that.

When we arrived Billy and I were given a can of soft drink and snacks were readily available. The object of the night, playing football, we thought, though we thought wrong, was to prepare medals to be presented to the boys at a forthcoming event. These medals were to be encased within a clear plastic setting. This was done in 3 stages. The bottom plastic had to be melted, coloured emerald green, mixed, and prepared before being poured into either a square, circular or oval mould and allowed to set. Once set, the medal was placed on top and once again allowed to settle into the soft plastic until hard and immoveable. Once at this stage a clear plastic was melted and poured into the mould encasing the medal which was of course clearly visible. When set, the entire assembly was tapped with a wooden spoon allowing it to fall from the mould, and it was now complete and ready to be handed over to one of the unsuspecting proud boys.

It was a long process and involved boiling water constantly. The room was incredibly hot and Torbett's insistence of also leaving the fire on at full and the windows closed was a strange decision to us, but we were certainly not in a position to question it. Midway through the night Torbett went into his bedroom and returned wearing only a pair of shorts. He handed me and Billy a pair of Celtic's Boys' Club shorts and told us to remove our trousers and shirts and put on the shorts. He didn't want us to get any of the molten plastic on our clothing apparently. We would also be able to cool down now!

We had over 200 medals to prepare and by the time we were finished we were incredibly tired, uncomfortably hot, and just wanted to get some sleep. Both lads had discussed and suggested sleeping in the lounge on the sofa, but Torbett said that was silly. We needed to get a good night's sleep and we could both sleep in his bed and he would sleep in the spare room.

Torbett suggested I and Billy go for a shower after him and we could then settle down for the night. We asked Torbett for our overnight bags which he had removed from the lounge at some point as we needed our pyjamas. Torbett told us the bedroom was very warm and we should just sleep in our shorts. Torbett went first, I followed with Billy showering last. When Billy was showering Torbett sat with me on the sofa with his arm around my shoulder. He made an attempt to get intimate with me and I asked him not to. I stood up and went over to the table for a snack for a few minutes, fortunately, we were joined fairly quickly by Billy, and the relief I felt on seeing him was inexpressible.

As we entered the bedroom Torbett suggested the smaller of us went into the middle as that would be more comfortable for everyone apparently. It became apparent the spare room had been forgotten and Torbett was sharing the bed with us. By quite a few inches I drew the short straw and I had to, unfortunately, sleep beside Torbett.

Torbett was quite right, the bedroom was

excessively warm and to compensate the blankets were removed just leaving a top sheet covering us all. I found it very difficult to sleep and recall, despite the trepidation I felt, being amused by the snoring coming from the left and right of me. I lay awake for a long time and considered getting up and going through to the lounge to sleep on the sofa. I was aware of Torbett's previous statement a few days before and feared his reaction would be one of anger and I certainly didn't want to do anything to anger him. It was uppermost in my mind that it was inconceivable for me to do anything that would give him a reason to tell my family what I had been doing. That would have crushed me and more importantly, crushed my mother.

I eventually fell asleep. I have no idea for how long but was suddenly awakened by a movement in the bed. The movement was in fact Torbett pulling me on top of him. He had placed his left leg under my legs and his right leg on top resulting in me being unable to move. As I awoke Torbett had his hand inside my shorts and was intimately touching me. He was masturbating as he was touching me and when he attempted to kiss me, I buried my face into his neck, so he was unable to do so. I tried to turn and remove myself from this scene and I told him to leave me alone. He ordered me to be quiet or I would wake Billy. The tone in his voice instilled further fear into me and I had no option other than to remain where I was until Torbett had finished. When he fell asleep, I cried but I cried quietly enough so that Billy wouldn't hear me, and his night wouldn't be disturbed.

I didn't sleep the rest of the night and as dawn broke, I got up quietly and went through to the lounge. I sat silently, tearfully, for several hours. My thoughts took an abrupt slap when I realised that although I was safe, Billy was still in there with Torbett. Was he OK? I tried to pluck up the courage to go through and make sure nothing was happening, but I couldn't, despite being worried for Billy. To interfere would have been career suicide so I decided, like the coward I thought myself to be, to remain where I was, and hope Billy was not being hurt. I was a coward!

The Devil and Billy came through and I was asked if I wanted scrambled eggs for breakfast as if nothing had happened. Billy asked me a couple of times if I was OK as he sensed something was wrong and I lied to him too, telling him I just wasn't feeling well. We had the eggs on toast for breakfast and immediately I finished it I went through to the bathroom and vomited.

Why Billy had been there I have no idea. Torbett as far as I know had made no advance towards him. Unless something had happened after I had gone into the lounge. Alternatively, it's possible he was indeed starting his deviant grooming process to abuse him sometime in the future. Maybe he was a target of the evil paedophile too!

Torbett dropped Billy off in the city centre for him to catch the bus home and drove me home to Drumchapel. For the very first time, there was complete silence during the journey despite him trying a couple of times to initiate a conversation about something, anything. He got no response. The one person who I had in my life to go to with my problems was now, by far, the actual problem and there was no route of escape. Torbett told me to tell my parents I had played in the match in Preston. He told me to say I had played and if I wanted, I could tell them I had scored two goals, he would confirm it if asked.

As I got home and went to my room, I convinced myself that I was now finished with Torbett, Celtic, and football. There was no way I wanted this to continue and without a second thought, I adapted my father's razor blades as a form of comfort to me regardless of what that activity could throw at me.

I spoke to mum and told her I wasn't happy at the Boys' Club and wanted to stop going. I told her I wasn't progressing and explained that I was never getting an opportunity to play. I couldn't see a future with Celtic and felt it better to stop going as that would also ease some tensions within the family. I wanted to be one of the lads who just disappeared.

As any mother would, she was having none of it. She lectured me about the importance of fighting for my place, never giving up and, rising to any challenge I came across in life.

The options I had were to tell her everything and never be a victim of Torbett's talons again or to continue the lie and spare her. I continued to lie and the following Thursday I unwillingly made my way to Celtic Park and to be in the company and in the control of evil people.

There was one other time I was abused at Torbett's Pinkston Road flat. Going home from training one night he told me he had something to collect from the flat. On our arrival, it was clear he wanted to take me into his bedroom. I bravely refused knowing that I really didn't have a choice should he force the issue as by this time I was becoming increasingly more fearful of the consequences should I go against his wishes. As we sat together, he surprisingly accepted I wouldn't go through to the bedroom with him, so he proceeded to sexually abuse me on the sofa.

After that, I ensured I was never alone with him in his flat again. He did try a few times to coax me to go with him, but I always steadfastly refused or waited in the car whilst he collected whatever he allegedly needed. There was, however, to be one more horrific attack that would set everything in motion to end my days and my abuse with Celtic's Boys' Club.

7. THE USA AND OTHER TRIPS

In 1968 we were scheduled for a USA trip. All the boys' passports and USA visas were obtained via the club, I cannot say for sure if Celtic Football Club or the Celtic's Boys' Club. In those days children shared their parents' passports, other than the annual ones available from the post office with only limited travel. There was an enormous feeling of pride with the boys that they all now had their first, very own passports. Having it come with a multiple entry visa for entry to the States was the icing on the cake. Even in those days, I would think, visas were not easily available, and here we all were with permission to go and see The Statue of Liberty as often as we liked until the visa expired. If the other lads were anything like me, it was viewed on an hourly basis and mine took pride of place in my bedroom. Positioned provocatively in view of my jealous brothers.

As you can imaging it was the major talking point between the boys and the officials for months beforehand. Plans were made, books were poured over containing photographs of our forthcoming destinations. Every team meeting or training session involved some sort of discussion about the trip. It certainly hyped the boys up and we couldn't wait to fly out.

Then the bombshell was announced at one team meeting a few weeks before departure.

The S.F.A. had stepped in and ordered Celtic to cancel the trip. We were given the reasons for the SFA actions of course, apparently the S.F.A. had discovered that the teams we were scheduled to play were not affiliated to the U.S.F.A. And as a result, the trip had to be cancelled in its entirety. There was no time to re-schedule games.

This reason was given to the boys by the Boys' Club officials themselves and we had no reason to question or doubt it amongst our extreme disappointment. Now, looking back and in consideration of events since, I have become very suspicious of their explanation for the cancellation.

I am sure this all took place after Jock Stein's son had left the club. It is my belief that it was Stein who did not want the trip to go ahead, and the decision had been nothing to do with the S.F.A. If Stein had had any inkling of abuse at the club at that time it would explain this momentous decision. A great deal of time and money had been invested in preparation for the trip and there really had to be a serious justifiable reason for its sudden cancellation. It hurt everyone terribly and lots of tears were shed that night. I doubt if any of the boys had previously experienced a disappointment like that and nor probably since. The opportunity of a lifetime had been snatched away from us at the very last moment. I did write to the SFA recently and requested information from them if there could have been any truth in these claims that they had been instrumental in the trip being cancelled but as I expected really, I received no reply.

My passport with the coveted USA visa was to become an important possession for me going forward but I was unaware of that at the time.

To ease our despondency, it was fairly quickly announced that we were to arrange another tour. We were to compete in a tournament in London which would include a four or five-day trip. This would involve a long, overnight, coach journey to Enfield in Middlesex. The name escapes me, but we were to be resident in a Catholic boarding school there or it may have been a monastery of some description, sorry I cannot be more sure of that. I do recall there being many Priests involved in our daily activities.

We were also to be the guests of Chelsea Football Club at one of their games at Stamford Bridge with stand tickets for and hospitality during and after the game itself. The tour, I would have thought, would comprise of competitive games considering it had been announced as a tournament? I cannot, other than daily training sessions, remember playing in, preparing for, or competing in any tournament, no-one kicked a competitive ball.

Daily training was the only time I slipped on my Adidas. I have no doubt that the reasoning behind the 'tour' was to remove vulnerable children from the umbrella of safety that was their families and to open up many situations where children could be manipulated and abused.

One thing that I can recall however had far more sinister undertones and despite trying to, on many occasions, clear my mind to remember events in greater detail I have been unable to do so. The lads had been accommodated in a dormitory of about 20 bunks. The officials had rooms adjacent. I have a memory of awakening one night in a room separate from the other boys. How I got there I have no idea; I certainly have no recollection of going there myself nor having been instructed by anyone to do so earlier in the evening. When I awoke and sat up, I did see Torbett and two Priests standing by the doorway. Once they realised, I was awake I was instructed to go back to the dormitory a few doors down. I cannot in all honesty recall anything else, I know I was not in pain and still had my Celtic shorts on, our normal sleeping attire. I returned to the dorm and slept. In the morning I discussed it with no-one. I was unsure if it had been an event or if I had been dreaming. To this day my recollection has not improved so I cannot make any accusations, nor can I write more as to do so would allow non-factual elements to be introduced into my story. I have however thought about that night often and sometimes I wished I could break into the memory for the answers I sought. Other times I was ever so thankful that the recollection remained out of bounds.

I recall going on the trip to Stamford Bridge the next day though the day itself is very much distant in my recollections. It has always made me question why such an important event in my past could so easily be forgotten. It has been.

Does this sound like a 'separate entity'?

8. THE TOY SHOP

A toy shop should be the ultimate joy for children. Joe's Toy Shop on the Maryhill Road became a living hell for me. To this day, I have feared going into toy shops, even with my own three children. I could never explain to them why I always wanted to leave and leave them disappointed.

Joe's Toy Shop, near to Queens Cross on the Maryhill Road in Glasgow was run by Joe Boyle. Boyle was also a Celtic's Boys' Club official at the time, I think he was the treasurer but can't be certain at this point.

I had been with Torbett quite a few times before and had visited with a couple of the other lads on occasions. Nothing special was ever done there though we were allowed to play with some of the faulty or unwanted but used goods that had been returned. There were always board games to occupy our time while Torbett and Boyle would discuss their concerns about whatever in the front shop. We were always asked, as much as possible to stay in the back room of the shop so customers would not be distracted from their purchases.

Only twice did I visit Joe's Toy Shop alone with Torbett when he had cash or paperwork to leave or collect. Torbett was always proud and revelled in showing off the amount of cash he often had. Hundreds of pounds in the sixties would equate to many thousands today. The second visit was to be my last visit and one of the last times I would be alone with my abuser.

It was a Saturday, and no game was planned but Torbett had instructed me to meet up with him at lunchtime in Dinos Restaurant. We had lunch and he had told me we were going to Joe's Toy Shop to work on a new line he was proposing selling in the shop to the kids, and to the many adults who would think a piece of cheap tat was appropriate to acknowledge a great victory in the Portuguese sunshine.

Torbett and I went up to the shop and it transpired their intention was to make up small replica plastic European Cups to be sold in the toy shop. Standing about four inches in height the cheap plastic Cup was set on a small black plastic plinth. It was my job to make strips from a Dymo Gun with the words Celtic F.C. Winners – 1967 onto green tape. The backing was removed, and the strips were cut and were then stuck to the plinth.

There were boxes and boxes of this rubbish that had to be worked upon. We had been doing so for an hour or so when Torbett took the last few out from the current box and told me to get another box from the back room.

As I did so I was followed and Torbett sat on the

table beside the boxes on a space presumably left available for the purpose that had been planned and was just about to expose itself, and him.

He put his arm around my shoulder and grabbed the back of my neck forcing me towards him. It really hurt. I was aware of what he was trying to do and despite my intense fear, my heart racing, and my instantaneous tears blinding me I denied him the opportunity to defile me. I clenched my teeth together and pursed my lips making his penetration impossible. His tightening grip on my neck was a sure indication he was ordering me to comply. I ignored the pain and continued to ensure he was unable to get what he wanted. I could feel him on the side of my face as he masturbated, and I wanted to vomit but it just wouldn't happen. Eventually, after what seemed like hours, Torbett finished, and he let go of my neck. 'Conveniently', there were tissues on the table, and he wiped the side of my face, smiling at me as he did so. I remember being disgusted at the smell of him on my face. To this day that smell, even that of my own, disgusts me and is a reminder of when that animal attempted to rape me.

I immediately turned and walked out of the shop, without looking back. As I left, Joe Boyle was still sitting beside the shop counter. I didn't look in his direction nor did he make any attempt to help an obviously distressed little boy leaving his shop to ask what was wrong. He must have known something untoward had happened on his premises that day but chose to ignore it for whatever reasons he may have had.

I was a long way from my home in Drumchapel. About 7-8 miles and I started to make my way home on foot. I turned many times to ensure Torbett was not following me, always prepared to either run or hide to avoid him. I was visibly upset, and many people glanced as I walked by, but no-one stopped me to enquire further except one kindly lady who asked if I was OK as I sat on a wall obviously in distress. I cannot remember the conversation other than her asking if I was OK and if I wanted her to phone my mum, but I do recall her smile, it helped. I had an old school mate who had moved from Drumchapel and was now living beside Anniesland Cross on the Great Western Road. I was about halfway on my journey, but I took this detour. I went to his house to seek some form of assurance that I was safe. He wasn't in, as I got no reply, I had no option other than to continue my way home myself. I did ensure though that I did not take the same route that Torbett had taken me many times and I went 'the long way round' to be sure of my safety.

By the time I got home several hours later I thought I was empty of tears. I had no more to give, but at least I was home, safe.
I went to bed as I didn't want anyone else to see

my distress. Sometime later mum came into my room to see if I was OK, and I pretended to be asleep. She knew I was awake probably but respected my space and left without saying a word. Before she left though, she gently lifted my head and replaced my pillow with a dry one.

9. STEIN'S DUMFRIES CHARITY GAME

After training one Thursday we were addressed by Torbett who had something of the utmost importance to announce because instructions had come down direct via the Celtic boardroom and from the 'big man' himself. Apparently the globally respected and admired, Jock Stein (Mr. Stein) had received a letter from a young, handicapped boy who attended a school in Dumfries. I believe it was a residential school but of that, I'm not certain. Unfortunately, neither can I remember the name of the school. The young lad had asked Mr. Stein if, the next time he came to a Celtic match at Parkhead, would he be allowed to see and hold The European Cup.

Mr. Stein, being the big-hearted man, he was (or was, in my eyes at that time, things changed) had written back and suggested we bring the cup to the young lad instead as his attendances at Celtic Park were expected to be few and far between. Mr. Stein had then phoned the school and had arranged for Celtic's Boys' Club under 14 team to travel to Dumfries and play a challenge match against the school. We would take the European Cup with us for the youngster to fulfil his dream. Additionally, it would surely have executed a few dreams for the Celtic Boys' too. We had of course seen the European Cup within the confines of its glass cabinet in the trophy room, but this was an opportunity for us to get up close, hold it ourselves, and not only that but hold it aloft whilst wearing the Hoops.

The match was all arranged for a Sunday a few weeks away and we were all asked to ensure our parents were happy for us to go on the trip. It meant an early start, our coach would leave Celtic Park at 9 a.m., and we would be returning to Glasgow late evening.

Hospitality had been arranged by a local hotel and kick-off was scheduled for 3p.m. That would allow the Celtic's Boys to spend a great deal of time with the school pupils and give them, hopefully, a boost before we returned to Glasgow.

We were all rewarded with a new pair of Adidas football boots from Torbett and were told we would be allocated full, new strips for the occasion. It was a great honour to have been selected as the team to represent Celtic Football Club with their charitable day out and looked forward to it immensely. The boys chatted about it between themselves as they changed to go home, and everyone was desperate to play and be involved in this special game. Particularly as it had been organised by Mr. Stein himself. You may wonder why 'Mr. Stein' and the formality of that? You were in deep trouble if you addressed him in any other way, boss, jock, gaffer, or anything else was just not tolerated. 'Mr. Stein' it had to be and in all my time there that rule applied to everyone, anyone, with absolutely no exceptions, even the Lisbon Lions respected it.

I spoke to my mum of course and there seemed to be no problem with the arrangements. She was also pleased that I had been selected to go and spoke about it quite a few times on the run-up to the allocated Sunday. The only question my father had for me was if it was a Catholic school we were going to. He couldn't understand why when I said I didn't know. It had never occurred to me to even ask and most certainly hadn't occurred to him that some people, including me, just don't care.

As it was a Sunday morning game, with an early start, I felt it appropriate for me to get my kit ready the night before and had decided on an early night to ensure I had enough sleep to give my best should I have been selected to play. I hadn't been selected to play in any previous competitive match. The subs-bench often but never the preferred team selection. This was a friendly game however and I had experienced playing in a few of those, so I was certainly hopeful. I ensured my green blazer was pressed, my shirt crisp and white, my tie and grey trousers ironed, and my shoes polished. I was ready.

I had to leave the house at 7.30 a.m. So, I set my alarm for 6.30 a.m. to ensure I was up and prepared in plenty of time.

My brothers were well aware of the importance of the next 24 hours but took it upon themselves to ensure I was kept up as late as possible. Sharing a room with them gave me no special rights, and they had as much entitlement to be there as I had. I think it was near midnight when my mother eventually had had enough and demanded they settle down for the night. When they allowed me to, I slept.

I awoke without the alarm having actually commanded me to do so. It was daylight and that was the signal that it wasn't too early to get up. I threw the covers back and had a look at the clock. It was 8.55 a.m. I felt horribly numb, surely, I hadn't slept through the alarm. It was then I realised the button had been pressed down, cancelling the 'Big Ben' alarm. Who the culprit was, who did this I'll never know as everyone, of course, laughingly denied it and blamed me for not setting it properly, "little fenian can't even set an alarm clock". I know it was the handy work of either, one of the bastards sharing my room or the bastard sharing my mother's bed. I never did find out for sure, so I just collectively blamed each and every one of the fuckers.

I was devastated, not just at missing the game itself but knowing I was going to go through absolute hell at the club for letting them down and, more importantly, letting Mr. Stein down in his special charity match. I went downstairs without bothering to get dressed and started to make my breakfast, well, the bowl of cornflakes that had become my comfort food.

I had only two telephone numbers to call in an emergency for Celtic Boys' Club. One was Torbett and the other for the Celtic Football Club's main reception. I was aware that Torbett would have already left his home to meet the coach, so I decided to phone Celtic Park to ask for a message to be somehow transmitted to him with my apologies. I waited until just after 9.30 and made the call. My call was answered almost immediately, and I made the young lady on the other end aware of my predicament. I was open and honest and told her I had slept in due to not hearing or alternatively not setting the alarm properly. I didn't mention anything about the bastards I shared a room with nor my bastard father. I apologised and asked her to get a message to Torbett via the school itself if that was at all possible.

It was shortly after 11 a.m. when a telephone call came into the Woods household. My elder sister answered and immediately summoned me to the hallway where the phone had its place, beside the Yellow Pages, and told me it was a Celtic secretary phoning for me. The caller was the lady I had spoken to earlier, and she asked if it was possible for me to get to St Enoch subway station for 12 noon? I said that I could. She told me a car would pick me up there to take me to the match in Dumfries.

I ran upstairs immediately and got dressed in my Celtic attire and grabbed my bag which contained my new kit and my new Adidas. It was then that I learned a valuable lesson of being prepared for any eventuality. Everything being prepared the night before was a bonanza. I was ready within a minute or two.

I asked my dad to take me into St Enoch which was in Glasgow City Centre. He refused. My heart sank again, and I can't describe the desperation I felt at that time. I couldn't possibly phone again to say I can't make it and there certainly wasn't enough time to go by public transport.

My sister saw the tears in my eyes, and she thankfully came to my rescue by offering to give me a ride into town. She had recently passed her driving test and had proudly invested in a used Rover 2000. I don't know if she loved me enough to care, just wanted to try the new car out again and wanted to show off, or just wanted to fuck my father off. I didn't care, though I would have much preferred the latter, I hugged her for her kind offer, and we were on our way.

It was 11.15 a.m. by the time we eventually got underway so only had 45 minutes to get to St Enochs. Being a Sunday, early morning, traffic was very light, and we made it comfortably with at least a good 10 minutes to spare. My sister, thankfully, hardly spoke at all on the journey. She asked me a little about the game itself but no more than that.

Looking back, it was probably a case of the less she knew the better for her. In any domestic blow-out, she could respond with her lack of knowledge and certainly a lack of interest so as not to get involved in their strategy. There had been many an issue domestically, but none had escalated into a full-blown sectarian war, just a few snide comments here and there with the occasional reference to my footballing ability and how if I was the standard Celtic would be taking into the next decade, it was, they told me often, all good news for Rangers Football Club and their fans.

We didn't have to wait long which was good as I had taken the decision to wait outside my sister's car in consideration, I did not know who and which car would be the one sent to pick me up. My sister waited patiently in her car, watching over me to ensure I would come to no harm. If only she had known the reality I'd have been dragged back into her car and never allowed near my Celtic family again.

The car arrived and gave a toot for my attention. I recognised the driver and his front-seat passenger immediately of course. I walked in amazement towards the car hardly daring to believe what I was seeing in front of me. The driver was none other than Mr. Stein and his passenger, Sir Bob Kelly, the Celtic Chairman. The car did not have a split-screen but was a beautiful piece of machinery. From memory it was a burgundy colour and seemed, to me, to be as big as a ship.

I gave my sister the thumbs up, blew her a kiss and she watched as we drove off after I had opened the back door of the ship and climbed aboard.

The mantra, "children should be seen and not heard" had been drilled into me over the years by most adults I had come into contact with. I utilised their advice on this extremely memorable trip to Dumfries and, kept my mouth shut. The journey was expected to take probably a couple of hours, and to be honest, my chest was bursting with pride to be in the company of, who I perceived then, to be two of probably the most famous men in British and perhaps European football at that time.

I watched Stein constantly via his rear-view mirror. Their conversations, of course, revolved around football. I was mesmerized with their knowledge of the game and in particular their apparent knowledge of all the European Clubs and European Players. I remember, thinking, it was simply probably their job to know? It still left a lasting impression and made me more aware of what my professional footballing career may well entail in the years to come.

Stein eventually caught my eye in the rear-view mirror and asked me what my last name was. I presumed he only knew me as Gordon and nothing else. I told him it was Woods. He thought for a moment and stated that there was not another professional player in the game with the surname Woods at that time. After a few moments, he corrected himself when he remembered a player who was playing for, I think he said, the English club Ipswich in their reserve team. His recall of players was absolutely amazing.

Stein then asked me what I thought was in the large wooden cabinet that was placed beside me on the other passenger seat in the back of the ship. I hadn't a clue of course and Stein invited me to open it. It had been closed with one simple, central, brass latch that swung over to secure the valuable contents. I swung the latch clockwise and attempted to open the doors. Space constraints forbade me to open it completely but sufficiently to allow me a close-up view of the European Cup. I dared not touch it; I was fearful of my fingerprints being transferred onto it for two reasons. It would detract from its majestic, superbly polished appearance but more importantly, if it was ever stolen my fingerprints would be on it! Here was the most valuable European Trophy in the back of a ship sailing, at speed, down the A74 and I was its temporary custodian. Proud as fuck!

That was the sum total of any talk between us. Sir Bob Kelly did not acknowledge my existence at any time during the journey. Maybe he knew I was a 'Proddie'? Stein was too but I didn't know that then.

We eventually arrived at the school and Torbett was there to meet the car with our teams 'Captain' and a few of the dignitaries from the school. As we all disembarked, no gangplank, fortunately, Torbett immediately turned to the captain (the team Captain not the ships!) and told him to accompany me to the changing rooms where he would speak to me later. Ominous!

10 minutes later Torbett came in took me to one side. I was already in my kit as I had been desperate not to keep anyone else waiting for any reason. We went through to a small side room beside the changing facility, (not the controversial one) and told me to prepare for the game as I was playing. This was after taking a bollocking for my tardiness. As I turned, overjoyed, to re-join my teammates, Big Jock, I can call him what the fuck I want now, stepped in front of me, and asked Torbett why I was already in my kit. "He's been selected", Torbett replied. The gaffer was raging, "Is he fuck, if he can't get up in time for an important match, he's

certainly not playing for us". I was devastated to say the least. Not just in not playing but also the fact I was kept well away from The European Cup for the rest of the day.

Stein turned and left without any further communication with me, verbal or non-verbal. The fact he had mentally destroyed me at 14-years-old, embarrassed me, and Torbett within the earshot of the team was of little importance. The discipline within the Boys' Club and perhaps Celtic, in general, took precedence to everything else for the Stein way, probably, partly a reason for his success. Who was I to argue with that? I changed from my kit and reflected on what might have been without the interference of the bastards at home still revelling, no doubt, in their success in slapping me down and making my life a little bit more distressing than was necessary. My team-mates didn't help, they had ignored me as I re-joined them compounding my sadness.

Jock Stein had wanted to teach me, Torbett, and every other player that day a lesson, and he had gone a long, long way out of his expected remit to do so. In the weeks and months to come, I understood him and fully respected what he had done and the way he did it. It was a lesson I was to remember my whole life, and to this day, tardiness is very much a pet hate of mine.

I can't remember the score that day though I am

quite sure we, sorry they, hammered them.

The coach journey back took much longer than my journey South. Midway through the trip where I had been sent to the back of the bus to sit by myself as an additional punishment, I took a cramp. I hadn't even played but had an agonising cramp. Probably being cooped up within a little area in the ship due to the European Cup taking space priority. The bus was stopped, and I was carried out onto the side of the road. The club physio massaged my leg to clear the cramp. Not the kind of massage we got at the controversial changing facility I must add but a proper one, from a proper physio. It worked and the rest of the journey was uneventful. I assumed someone had arranged the cramp as a punishment for having disappointed 'Big Jock'.

On arrival back at Glasgow I was immediately ordered by Torbett to go home by public transport whilst the other lads had a bit of a party at Celtic Park and a fleet of taxis took them home. I was hoping the number 64 to Glasgow Central would go via anywhere rather than its direct route. I was in no hurry to get home. I was desperately upset on the journey. I had noticed quite a few quizzical looks from fellow passengers with one lady asking me if I was, OK? I confided in her and admitted that I had been sent home for my transgression. She sympathised and suggested I get home as soon as I could to the support of my family. Yeah? You haven't a fucking clue lady, I thought.

When I did arrive home, I fucked everyone off, even mum, their questions went unanswered. I went to bed and tried to fall asleep.

Bastards!

Does this sound like a 'separate entity'?

10. CELTIC'S BOYS' CLUB V ST BENEDICTS

Celtic Park • 14th September 1968 • Attendance 69,561

The above date should have been etched into my mind as one of my proudest moments. An occasion for me to speak about to my children and grandchildren in the years to come. To speak about it with pride, a sense of achievement, and fond memories would have been wonderful, and a cherished part of my childhood. Instead, of course, from what you're about to read, it was a memory I cast to the deepest recess I could find in a feeble attempt to distance myself from the horrors I had faced.

I would talk later to friends, even family perhaps about that day at Celtic Park having happened but not that I was involved and what had occurred at it. The day was one straight out of any boy football comic book. As a 14-year-old, with all my 14-year-old teammates we were about to experience what no-one in our age bracket had experienced before, nor probably since, in the history of the beautiful game, this was indeed a one-off, never to be repeated, never to be forgotten. But it was a memory that was deemed superfluous by me to ensure my well-being and my fragile mental health, until now.

Celtic's Boys' Club under 14's had reached a Cup Final. I can't remember which, at that age, and with the system then, you were involved in many Cup Finals every season, some of value, some not. Our opponents were to be another Glasgow youth side, St Benedicts. As always, Celtic's Boys' Club were the overwhelming favourites to lift the trophy and we could not be seen to let our Club down if we were to retain our justified respect amongst our peers throughout Scotland as representatives of Celtic Football Club.

The previous season there had been horrific scenes of violence during and after the earlier couple of 'Old Firm' games. Particularly after the match when riots, fighting, severe violence, and civil disobedience had prevailed from London Road to the Paisley Road West and all points in between. Abhorrent scenes.

The two clubs, Celtic and Rangers, together with the S.F.A. and the Glasgow Police convened a meeting to discuss a forthcoming League encounter at Celtic Park between the two clubs. Their objective was to try and find solutions to reduce, even slightly, though preferably substantially, or indeed eliminate the problems that had marred the previous games. The came up with a host of proposals, most of which just was not feasible. The one that they deemed to be the front-runner was that at the final whistle the Celtic fans would be kept in the stadium for 30-45 minutes after the game and the Rangers fans would be emptied out onto London Road to make their way home on a fleet of number 64's to Glasgow Central. This would avoid the two sets of supporters mingling because, regardless of who won or lost, the hatred would always be there, just transferred to the failures on that particular day.

Of course, caging the Celtic fans for that period of time was not going to go down well with the home support. Stein, who attended the meeting then came up with an idea that was hailed as brilliant by the other attendees and so the solution was found, and the stage was set.

The Celtic fans would still be kept within the stadium for 30 – 45 minutes after the main 'Old Firm' game, however, as entertainment, to keep them occupied and to avoid the anticipated pies, fists, and Molotov throwing, the Celtic Boys' Club would play their Cup Final against St Benedicts with the hope that the Celtic fans would be happy to stay behind to watch the future stars of Celtic collect another trophy and the Rangers fans would go home.

Stein himself made the announcement after a training session at Barrowfield to the boys. There was uproar in the facility with no-one really daring to believe what they had just heard. It was obvious the Boys' Club officials were as excited as any of the players who could just not grasp the reality of the situation, they were to play their final on the turf at Celtic Park. I reminded them all not to be late!

The big day came, and the excitement was immeasurable. We had to be at Celtic Park for 1.30 p.m. We met at the changing facility and as a group at 2.15 p.m. we were led through the main doors of Celtic Park and taken to our seats in the stand, I do not recall how many boys were there, but I certainly was, with Jim Torbett, in the main Celtic Stand. We were to go and change for the match midway through the second half so as to be ready to take the field at 4.45 p.m. To be in the stadium, not as a spectator, not as a visitor, not as a guest but as an actual player, about to play in a cup final, can you imagine? No, of course, you can't, neither could we. The dream continued.

With the score at 1-2 in Rangers favour we were signalled to make our way to the changing room within the stadium. As we stood up to make our way-out Rangers scored their third indicating a very fast exit was now required. As we exited the stand making our way down the stairs an enormous cheer went up again. We didn't know which team had scored until we turned and noticed one of the stewards dancing a jig at the top of the stairs. 2-3 confirmed.

To be honest the score line at the time was of little importance. Although we were all Celtic's Boys with Celtic hearts, we had other things on our mind. We were about to follow our heroes representing Celtic Football Club at Celtic Park in front of a full house. If they should lose, we would make up for it by taking the trophy to the delight and in front of 10's of thousands of our most fervent followers.

A few minutes before the final whistle we were called upon to line up in the tunnel. Celtic tightly to the right, St Benedicts tightly to the left to allow for the players to exit the pitch and have free access to their respective changing rooms. We had our minds focussed on the job ahead, as we had been trained to do, concentration was of the utmost importance. That obligatory focus was blown to bits when the unimaginable happened.

As the players started up the tunnel with a bit of jostling and pushing, nothing serious though, Mr. Stein was seen to approach the referee angrily, pointing his finger into the referees face he declared "You knew what the score was going to be before you set foot on that fucking park", the referee ignored the comment, and the finger and continued forward as other officials restrained Stein. It was all over in seconds, but it certainly had a serious effect on the youngsters preparing for the biggest match of their lives. Such a pity the shameful incident occurred in front of the boys. It unsettled us and for the first few minutes of our own match, it was on our minds. Of course, as Celtic players, we pulled ourselves together and got on with the job at hand. I say we; I really mean they as I was, surprise, surprise, on the bench!

What was not anticipated and came as a complete shock to all the officials from Celtic, the S.F.A. and the Police was the fact they hadn't accounted realistically for Rangers being victorious that day, except Rangers of course. The result had been, 2-4 in their favour so of course, their support was having a party. Not only having a party but they decided to have it in Celtic Park. They weren't going anywhere! Their plan had failed, the big man's brilliant idea had let everyone down. The Rangers fans had a whole 45 minutes to stay and humiliate their opposing fans and they sure did it in style. Not only did they refuse to leave as was the desired result, but they also took it upon themselves to stay and support St Benedicts. There's a huge, comical, irony there if ever there was one! I suppose they hadn't quite grasped that St Benedicts were a Catholic Club!

As we took to the field Celtic Park had lost no-one. The full complement of 69,561 spectators remained to welcome the teams onto the park. Actually, the true figure was probably 69,559 as my father and uncle left on the final whistle as neither wanted to watch one of their own wearing the Hoops, they were ashamed.

It overwhelmed the boys, and the event was way too much for some of them to handle. The noise, a cacophony, was distracting and frightening to the kids. For any 14-year-old, on both sides I must add, to face the aggression towards them on that day was a disgrace. In the early stages, it was relentless. It did calm down during the first half. I can only surmise that common sense prevailed, and they realised just who they were aiming their verbal abuse at, children. The kids handled it after a while and their only complaint post-game was, they couldn't hear their teammates or even the whistle on the park itself.

The game was over in a flash. By full time many in the crowd had left although still a fantastically huge audience for a Celtic's Boys' Club game, I would estimate at 20,000+. I think we only played 20 minutes duration for each half. The Celtic's Boys' Club ran out 4-2 winners and lifted the trophy in front of an appreciative crowd at Celtic Park. The boys were all given a commemorative plaque. My own plaque was to disappear from my family home for it only to resurface, in heart-breaking circumstances, 30 years later. More on that to come.

One thing that really angered me that day was the fact I had been given two stand tickets for the match to give to my parents. My dad of course took one and I think one of my uncles accompanied him. No major issue with that, however, that night the match was on T.V. The family were watching and as the main Celtic v Rangers game finished, and the boys ran onto the park, my father immediately turned the TV off and I missed watching the report of the Celtic

Boys' Club Cup Final. I wanted to watch it desperately and he couldn't give a fuck.

That played on my mind for a very long time. I couldn't understand why there was no pride shown by anyone in my family, at the time, as one of their own ran onto the Parkhead turf to have the chance to represent the current European Champions. It certainly defied belief and hurt me tremendously. I eventually cast what happened to the back of my mind. Other events at Celtic's Boys' Club took precedence in screwing up my view on life.

I stated at the start of this chapter that that day should have been etched into my mind as one of my proudest moments. It wasn't. After the match, Torbett ran me home and 100 yards from safety he stopped the car, as was usual, and I sat, disconnected, staring at the streetlamp over my fathers' car once again as he did what he wanted. It left me desperate to forget that particular 14th September. It had never existed, and I had never been there.

When I came forward as a child abuse victim and released the details of this occasion it was evident that prior to this the legal team and press had been unaware of it. They viewed it with great interest as it partly ridiculed Celtic's stance of being a separate entity as early as 1968.

Match Programme explaining the game that apparently never happened!

Celtic, I have been told, had no recollection of the game when asked by journalists following the release of my story. Fortunately, a journalist and my legal team have discovered, I believe, the archived original minutes taken when the two Clubs, the SFA, and the Police had their meeting. Video evidence of the kid's game itself has also now also been unearthed to prove their stance delusional. The match is well recorded in the Celtic View, arranged by, and commented on in Jock Stein's own column, newspapers, media, and in the official match day programme. In fact, the game was called "The Safety Game". Safety and Celtic should never be used in the same sentence.

Does this sound like a 'separate entity'?

11. MY DREAM CRASHES

The abuse continued and Torbett seemed to gain confidence in his brazenness and its frequency. His abuse had become more aggressive and hurt many times, but I dare not complain, my mum's sanity depended on my silence.

I was lost but had accepted that this was what was probably required to make it in football. Everything I was enduring was probably normal and I had thoughts of the Lisbon Lions going through the same as me when they were children. I felt sorry for them but look at them now? I'm sure it was all worth it to them now that they had become the Kings of Europe.

Torbett continued to promise me that one day I would get my chance in the Boys' Club team but that I just wasn't quite ready yet. Other than the occasional game in friendlies, I had been kept on the side-lines or the bench but still hadn't played a competitive game wearing the hoops.

One thing that gave me hope was that there appeared to be fewer and fewer lads at training. When I first entered The Celtic family there were possibly 30 young lads being prepared for the fame that they all desperately wanted. Now there were maybe 24. Some lads left and didn't seem to be replaced immediately. Some went and others started but not in the same numbers as before. because of this my chances of actually getting a game were increasing.

One evening at training Torbett told me he was unable to drive me home and that I should leave training a bit earlier so I could be home in time as I would have to use public transport. He had something else to do that night apparently. I wasn't too worried about leaving early but he insisted I go 30 minutes before the rest of the lads after giving me a few quid for my fares. I was a bit upset at leaving early but comfortable and relieved that, for a while anyway, I didn't need to endure the discomfort of fixing my gaze on my new best friend, the fading streetlight standing proudly safeguarding my dad's car, and me.

The following week Torbett avoided me most of the night which in itself wasn't unusual as he often had many other things to do. When it was time to go Torbett told me to clean up some of the kit lying around, bag them for the laundry, change, and come out to his car when I was ready.

I did what was requested and got ready to leave for the night. When I got to the car a back door was open for me to get in. Another of the lads was sitting in the front with Torbett which strangely made me feel a little jealous. That was my seat and had been for over a year. Despite the horrors of that seat, it was mine!

I have recently been in touch with the son of the seat's occupant that night and will respect his and his father's request that he not be named. My heart really goes out to him along with my sincerest best wishes as I'm well aware of what the poor kid would have gone through after that night. He was to be given an opportunity 55 years later that he bravely took, more on that to come.

As I sat in the back Torbett turned to face me and told me my time at the Boys' Club and our 'friendship' had come to an end. Confused at first as it was so unexpected, I questioned what he meant. On reiterating, he coldly looked straight into my eyes and told me I was finished. I was not allowed to come back to the Boys' Club. I could keep my uniform but would not be allowed to attend the training again.

My stomach fell to my feet and the tears filled my eyes as I made an effort to understand just what was happening. I was being thrown out of the club, never to be a lion, my time as a cub had come to an end I hadn't been selected. My emotions took over and I was very upset. I was sobbing as my seat's occupant turned to look at me. His blonde hair and striking blue eyes will remain in my memory forever. He was taking my place as Torbett's mentee. It was him and not I who would pull on the Hoops at a Cup Final.

I asked to go back into the hall and talk about it, but Torbett told me no. I tried to calm down but couldn't. I took deep breaths but that didn't help. Eventually, after no more than a few minutes, I was told it was time to go. I got out of the car and closed the door. Torbett drove off leaving me in the Celtic Football Club's car park without even a glance back. The heartless bastard had left a kid of 14-years-old who had just seen every dream he had ever dreamt disintegrate in a matter of a few, unpredictable minutes to fend for himself, distressed and destroyed. How could anyone do that to any child? Torbett could, but then again, his depravity and heartlessness towards children were a common occurrence. It would though take decades of being concealed, covered-up, enabled, and assisted before he faced exposure.

I stood and watched him drive onto London Road. I had the kit, the blazer, the tie, the grey trousers, and the shiny black shoes but I was no longer a part of the Celtic family and my dreams had been shattered by the man I trusted most in life.

I sat on the wall of the school beside Celtic Park and sobbed my heart out. Three or four no 64s came and went before I courageously took one to the city centre and went home. As I boarded, I took a final look at the stadium from which I was now outlawed, not allowed to be a part of. I had no idea why. Torbett's explanation in its entirety were the words he uttered in the car. Nothing else was said, no reasons given. I cannot recall exactly what happened when I got home and told my family what had occurred that night. What I do remember was that it wasn't memorable. Nothing much was said. My mother ran me a bath and my father sat in his chair saying nothing. My brothers were silent and gave me neither their support nor their ridicule. Their silence was deafening but not as deafening as my own screams within.

What had happened, and why did I deserve what Torbett had done to me. I couldn't work it out nor could I turn to anyone for an explanation or comfort. My pain was my own and for the first time in my life, I could confide in no-one. My mother had to be spared from the torment I was feeling, my father and family were totally unapproachable, and my friend of the past year who always had an ear to listen had discarded me without a care in the world.

I had to work out all the why's myself and it would be another 30 long years before that final piece of information to fit this particular jigsaw would be made available to me. In a future chapter I will recount an experience when the events of that night could and were explained to me by my mother and it all snapped into place.

My abusive nightmare was ending I thought but in reality, it was just the beginning. The road ahead was to be difficult, as difficult perhaps as that already experienced to date. When you cannot forget, the nightmares still take hold and manifest themselves to hurt as much as they can.

The devil's greatest trick is to convince people that he does not exist. He most certainly does, I had met him, faced him, in 1967, 1968 and I would face him again in 2023.

My dream had crashed, I was awake, and the dream had ended, I was alone.

12. THE SAN SIRO

By this time, of course, my complimentary tickets from Celtic's Boys' Club had come to an end. One of Celtic's most important games in their history was looming. Leeds Utd v Celtic in the European Cup semi-final. Billed as The Battle of Britain the English press had already written Celtic off before a ball was kicked. Of course, Don Revie's Leeds were flying high and were a magnificent team in those days so their disrespect could be understood, but only to a point. I doubt even many Celtic fans were confident in securing the win that would see them march on to the Final, to the San Siro in Milan.

I awoke on a Sunday morning, no-one had interfered with my alarm clock, and headed to Celtic Park for the ticket sales. Such was the huge demand for tickets the return game was moved to Hampden Park. There were quite a few turnstiles open and the crowd, although big, was orderly and I had been able to secure my two enclosure tickets within the hour. Once you were through the turnstiles with your tickets you only had to walk round to exit via the large corner side doors to get back into the car park area. As I did so I noticed another turnstile was about to open with no-one waiting in the queue, so I immediately took my chance and ran to the front and within minutes had managed to secure another two terracing tickets. Believe it or not, as I retraced my steps the exact thing happened at another turnstile with a 'Stand Tickets Only' sign being displayed outside. I guiltlessly took my opportunity once again.

When I caught the number 64 to Glasgow City centre, I was the proud owner of 6 valuable tickets for 3 different parts of the stadium. More than I'd ever been allocated by the Boys' Club!

On arriving home, and announcing my news, my father and the other Protestants in my household suddenly declared they were going to do the Scottish thing and thought 'the right thing to do' was to wish Celtic well in their semi-final and lend them their temporary support. I saw through all the bullshit of course but to keep the peace the tickets were immediately allocated to my father and his brother, my two brothers, who were still at home, and I kept two for myself and a mate. Fucking vultures. I did add a couple of quid to each ticket to 'cover expenses'. No-one had even thought to ask me where the money had come from for me to secure the tickets, so I did not have to confess to the crime committed several days earlier.

Celtic had won 1-0 at Elland Road in the first leg with a goal after just 90 seconds from a young George Connolly. I listened to the radio alone. No-one else in the house was the least bit interested. The press was stunned. Excuses were manufactured but they still couldn't change the totally unexpected result that night.

Being such a huge game, it was moved from Celtic park to Hampden Park. With 136,505 tickets having been sold, that was the attendance expected at Hampden for one of its greatest games ever. Again, the English press had put the first leg down as a fluke result and fully expected Revie's magnificent men to overcome their inferior challengers on the night. The double steel exit gates at the four corners of Hampden were breached that night and unofficial estimates were that 150,000+ were crammed into Hampden Park. The history books now show that Leeds were humbled that night with Celtic winning 2-1 and 3-1 on aggregate. Celtic were indeed marching on to the San Siro Final.

I was determined to go to that final. I had to send off for my tickets by post. Within a week of doing so, I received my two tickets for the final in Milan. My father, and surprisingly my mother had refused to give me permission to go. I was 15 years old and had intended to hitchhike the 1200 miles to Milan. Both realised with my history of disappearing they had really no chance of keeping me chained at home. They knew that I would go, with or without their permission. After a fair bit of discussion, they later relented and agreed for me to go as long as I was accompanied by my 18-year-old brother. We prepared our baggage and when the time was right my brother, and I started our journey.

The first leg was a coach to London, and we had promised our parents that we would not hitch-hike and had enough money to get there via coach and train after my mum had given her donation. We did have enough, to get there but not to get back. We would cross that bridge once we were European Champions again. The second leg on the journey was the train from Victoria Rail Station to Dover and the cross-channel ferry to Calais. As the ferry was preparing to dock in Calais, I was sitting at the bar finishing my coke waiting for my brother who had gone to the toilet. The bartender was cashing up and the till was open. He was called to the back of the bar for something, and I grabbed the opportunity. My hand darted into the till and grabbed a handful of notes, like Oliver Twist I was off amidst the crowds waiting to disembark. I called on my guardian as he returned and disappeared from the sight of any watching, revengeful eyes. We had enough to get home now probably.

We got as far as Lake Como in Italy a day or two before the match. We booked into the youth hostel that was over-run by fans from both sides. We were a bit concerned about what we were confronted with when we first arrived in Italy. There was a national strike in the country at that time and the police were on strike. The army had been called in to ensure law and order and it was a bit worrying seeing the soldiers with their machine guns patrolling the streets. It certainly kept the two sets of fans in order.

So, there I was, excited beyond belief and not really understanding how it was possible for me to have made it all the way to the San Siro in Milan, to be one of the very few to have ever had the honour of attending and watching a European Cup Final live, actually there, in the crowd. How many 15-year-olds could boast that?

I had never experienced anything like it. The stadium wasn't full, but the noise dictated that it was, twice over! Big Tommy Gemmell scored the opener which resulted in an uproariousness from the traveling Celtic support. The feelings we were encountering at that moment were inexpressible. I had never experienced that excitability in my lifetime. It was to be short-lived however with the equaliser coming within a few minutes from Rinus Israel.

The first half concluded with the score at 1-1, I relaxed a little and I feasted on the atmosphere and the amazing scenes of the San Siro that were alien to most 15-year-olds. That was about to change, horrifically.

During the second half my young heart took the most horrendous dive. There, in my eye line, was Jim Torbett! I was in shock, Was it really him? I turned again to look and make sure but couldn't place him amongst the crowds, but the damage had been done. I began to feel nauseous. As I dropped into my seat my stomach collapsed and my heart rate increased to what could only have been dangerous levels without me being aware of it. My head began to spin, and I physically vomited. I cannot remember, to this day, most of the rest of that match. My brother looked at me with disgust and accused me of being a "drunken fenian bastard". I hadn't had an alcoholic drink and he should have known that.

I had to ask my brother on the way back to our hotel to confirm the final score. He looked at me with disbelief, shook his head, and walked off in his own direction leaving me to sit by myself in one of the many magnificent squares in Milan. I sat on the edge of a fountain that had been taken over by Celtic fans. There were both Celtic and Feyenoord fans in the square, all interacting and having a great time together, there appeared to be no ill-feeling between the two sets of supporters. Celtic had been outplayed and everyone had accepted that.

The next thing I remember I was being carried through the square by four strangers. Two had my feet and two held my arms. Where they were taking me, I had no idea but suddenly my brother appeared with other Celtic fans and released me from their capture. They were four Italians. Their intentions remain a mystery, but I was saved.

We returned to our hotel and settled in for the night. I couldn't sleep, memories of the abuse flashed back into my fragility. I could not deflect them however hard I tried, so I cried. Softly enough not to be heard but even if I had been it would, no doubt, have been put down to my team's lack of success. Eventually, I kind of slept, intermittently, through the nightmares.

I woke up the next morning, the 7th of May 1970, knowing that was the last Celtic game I would ever attend. My love for Celtic had been ripped from me and I was later to learn many other aspects of my young life would be ripped from me also leaving me alone, misunderstood, secretive, and with many new traits that were forced uninvited into me by the abusive experience I had suffered, suffered at the hands of Torbett. It appeared he was free to wander the streets of Europe just like all the innocent people do. He wasn't innocent and should not have been allowed to wander anywhere? He should have been locked up with all the other sinister people who disgrace the human species, rapists, murderers, and child abusers.

Feyenoord lift the European Cup after beating Celtic 2-1 –
6th May 1970

On the way home my brother and I started to hitch-hike despite our promise to mum not to and despite my unexpected windfall on the ferry, we had massively over-spent and had barely enough for food for the journey.

We had started through Germany and had stopped for a bite to eat in-between lifts. Something caused an argument; I can't remember what that was, but it was severe enough for my brother to opt to give me a slap across the jaw. "Fuck off you little fenian bastard" my guardian suggested.

There was little I could do at that moment in time with regards to my religion but to "fuck off" was certainly a viable option. So "fuck off" I did! I walked off, collecting and swinging my haversack over my shoulders as I left. Crusty dry bread and ham in hand determined to make my violent guardian suffer.

After crossing over a bridge, I dropped down the steep embankment onto an Autobahn that was going somewhere, not in the direction we needed to go but I couldn't have cared less. I just wanted to distance myself from my attacker and did so laughing all the way. As I started to hitch-hike, I could see my brother starting to collect his belongings and come after me. There was no way he could announce, on his arrival home, that he had misplaced me somewhere in Germany! He dropped down the same steep embankment and started to run towards me just as a very considerate German gentleman stopped his VW Beetle and offered me a lift. He was heading for Stuttgart, and I quickly calculated that was a destination that would suit me fine. I climbed aboard and as we drove off, I gave my brother a cheery wave from the passenger window.

Stuttgart was a city that I recollected was the nearest to Waiblingen. S.K.V. Waiblingen was the youth team that we had welcomed to Glasgow a year prior. I decided to head to Waiblingen and look up one of their players, Gerhard (surnames aren't needed), who I had been writing to now and again. So, finding myself in a dangerous position the contacts that

I had made at Celtic Boys' Cub came to my aid.

I arrived in Waiblingen a few hours later and started to look around. I remembered that the coach of the youth team had said he had owned a Petrol Station in the town. I had been dropped off just outside town and walked into the town centre. I saw the railway station and immediately opposite was a Texaco garage, I tried my luck there. Bingo. The coach was stunned, of course. I explained I had been at the European Cup Final and had run out of cash to get home, I needed his help. He took me to stay with him, his wife, and their young daughter for a few days until arrangements could be made to return me home to Scotland. I believe he eventually contacted Celtic Football Club, who was able to give him my parent's information as I had conveniently forgotten my home phone number. Anyway, arrangements were made for me to be returned to Glasgow on the train a couple of days later. Who paid for that? I didn't ask, never have asked as it was, and still is, an irrelevance. It certainly wasn't a few years later when funds were needed to return me from California. My parents had 6 kids and my father wasn't exactly on any upper pay scale, my return home at that time was funded, I was told, by Celtic Football Club.

The funniest thing about it all was the day I was leaving I was sitting, enjoying the bustle of the German town, outside the Texaco Garage on its boundary wall devouring an ice-cream of some description. Who did I see sauntering up past the railway station? Yip, my orange guardian. He had guessed I would head to Waiblingen as he had been aware of the connection I had with the town, their youth team, and some of their players. He had checked where my selected Autobahn was heading and put two and two together. It was with the greatest of pleasure I told him I was going home by train. I gave him the last £10 I had (at least that's what I told him) to assist him on his journey... alone. As he walked off, I completed his humiliation by simply shouting "Fuck off, you big orange bastard"! He refused to acknowledge my shout and did not look back, he heard me though, I was certain.

13. AUSTRALIA BECKONS

I was having difficulty in my everyday survival. The horrible, disgusting thoughts and feelings within me would go nowhere. I desperately wanted them to go but they remained, convincing me to get the revenge I felt the perpetrator of my distress deserved.

I was now nearing 16 years old. I had great difficulty sleeping as I often refused its invitation. I knew as soon as I slept, Torbett might join me, for the sole purpose of abusing me again, killing my belief in life, slowly. I needed a way out.

I was getting more and more aware of my need to do something crazy. I recall imagining me with a weapon, a gun, a knife, doing something so severe that maybe I would be able to open up and tell someone because I would least have an opportunity to talk, and to be listened to. I couldn't tell anyone in my family, but my conscience was telling me to tell someone, anyone, other than my family, if only just to ease my guilt and release me from this captivity.

I read in a Sunday newspaper about a new opportunity for young people in Britain. The British Boys' Movement was encouraging young individuals to apply to emigrate to Australia. It seemed young, new blood was needed there to assist the country in its growth. There was a mass emigration there by adults, and families of course, at that time of course but this was an opportunity for young teens to travel alone to be a part of a new Australia.

I sent away for information and a week or two later the pack arrived at Harelaw Avenue with the brochure detailing how it would work and how to apply. I quickly hid the letter in my room as I was aware of my every move being closely monitored by the rest of the family. What they knew, I don't know but they knew something was not as it should be. I was never asked; I think my parents were happy to sweep it under the carpet. Since then, it has been swept under so many carpets, by so many people, individuals, Celtic, media, organisations, MPs, and all our governments, it's a repulsive, national disgrace.

My dreams of a career in the R.A.F., as an author or a vet, blew up in my face. Years of planning had become obsolete now that I had been forced into the decision to leave my education process and miss out on any attempt to gain passes in the 'O' and 'A' levels in examinations that would have been required to progress further. I declined the offer of another year at school to sit those exams and planned my escape instead. Without those qualifications, I was destined to become a failure and I didn't care. I needed to get away and that was my only thought at the time.

I ensured the application was completed

correctly and sent it away with my passport which had been obtained with courtesy from Celtic or its Boys' Club. To be honest for a long time I gave the application little thought. I had managed to get an office job working for a large Scottish Brewery in Port Dundas Street, Glasgow, and started my career though I continued supplementing my £6 a week wage with dubious pastimes. I was eventually sacked from there for trying to off-load stolen car radios to my colleagues. I'm really not proud of that!

When advised on return from the brewery one day that a letter had arrived for me, I was surprised. Mum wanted to know what it was about as the enveloped displayed the logo of the British Boys' Movement and of course not many letters dropped through our letterbox to the children. She refused to let me open it by myself and insisted on sitting with me as I did so.

The letter indicated I had provisionally been accepted for the movement. I was so excited though my mum didn't share any of it. We discussed the implications for a long time. She persistently asked why I was so determined to go, and I couldn't answer her honestly. Every time she asked the question the memories stabbed at me as I fought to find a reason that would justify me leaving my whole life behind. Friends, parents, bastard brothers, loving sisters, my life, would all be left behind, without a doubt, if I could or would want to be introduced to them ever again. We concluded our conversation by agreeing to hold a family meeting as soon as we could get everyone together.

As it turned out the meeting was convened with just my parents. My brothers had expressed their opinion that I could do whatever the fuck I wanted as far as they were concerned. They were of course oblivious to my reasons though I am quite sure it would have made no difference even if they knew. My sister was working, it seemed, constantly as an air traffic controller and my younger not deemed old enough to have an opinion.

My father was surprisingly calm, and my mother was unsurprisingly distraught. It was a very emotional time for me too though I managed to keep the horrors from being discovered and I concealed them well. I fought my corner well, too well at times as every time I scored a win, on each point, my mum only managed to distress herself even more than she had been previously.

We reached a majority at the end of the night two to one. My father's desire to give his permission for my travels to Australia outweighed his understanding of what it would do to mum. He probably just didn't care either way, for me or mum. Mum did not want to continue our meeting. She retired to her bedroom and left my father and me to complete the additional forms that were sent together with the parental consent documents.

The following day I personally ensured everything was posted as I certainly couldn't trust either of the adults involved to do so.

A few weeks passed, seemed like months and I received the acceptance on another of those, few and far between, sunny mornings in Scotland. I had been accepted to travel and the documents attached gave the details of my trip and where I was to be resident in Australia. I was going to Brisbane, by ship! A ship much bigger than Jock Stein's ship. The journey was to take 6 weeks and I was expected to assist on-board with whatever the purser deemed necessary.

It was still a long way off though, 8 weeks until I departed from Southampton. From that day to this I have never experienced time dragging the way it did then. It was horrific. Not as horrific as other elements of my young life but horrific none-the-less.

Eventually, my departure day neared, I had left my new job with a car parts supply company in Allison Street and packed everything I needed except a razor. Not that I feared self-injuring myself, purely because I was not in need of one just yet. I had said my farewells to everyone and anyone who mattered out with my household. I was ready to put my life-to-date somewhere, anywhere other than my future, and anticipated being free from my abusers forever.

My family arranged a night out as a farewell a few days before I was due to take the train to Southampton. I honestly cannot remember who all was there nor can I remember much of the night itself other than the heart-breaking events that were to expose themselves to me on our return home.

We had returned and I was relaxing in the lounge. Dad had gone out, we later discovered to see his mistress. My young sister screamed from the top of the stairwell something about mum. I raced to her bedroom, and she was in bed, unresponsive. We could not waken her at all, and she looked terrible. An ambulance was called, and my mum was rushed to the Victoria Infirmary. We were devastated, again.

We were told that mum was in a diabetic coma and although her condition was severe, she would be OK, given time. It all became evident in the days ahead that mum had been deliberately drinking too much. Not only that but her preferred drink that night was Carlsberg Special Brew, poison for a diabetic as mum was.

Was it an attempt to take her life or was it a cry out for me to cancel my plans? I never found out as I didn't enquire. It did scupper my plans however and the whole trip was cancelled, or at least put on hold until mum recuperated and was discharged from hospital a few weeks later.

I don't know if there was a connection, but my nightmares and memories returned with a vengeance. I was desperate for them to stop but now it appeared they would be with me forever.

Would I ever be free of them, could I let any circumstance commit me to a life of horror, or should I do whatever was required to get them to stop?

The next few weeks were horrendous, and I loathed Jim Torbett even more than I loathed myself.

14. MY WORLD TOUR

Now that my Australia adventure dream had been destroyed, I was determined to seek a satisfactory alternative. I still had to get away from everyone and everything. My head was in a crazy place, and I was really beginning to fear that I was going to do something unthinkable, to end my pain. I had started to self-harm by cutting myself with my father's razor blades. I would put my hands into as hot a sink full of water that I could stand and cut myself. I always cut the inside of my thumb; I could hide that with a clenched fist. My older brother's blades were there too but I got much more satisfaction using my fathers. I would notice that as the days progressed so did the level of my self-abuse. I was cutting deeper and deeper. One day I'm going to go too far I amused myself with, and I'll deserve it. Those thoughts, now looking back, horrify me that any child, could have been or will be, subjected to them.

Over a period of a few days, I collected everything together that I would need to make a break and get away from everyone. Mostly to get away from my memories of the abuse but of course, family and friends were all a part of those memories, and I was unable to separate them. All the money I had saved, my passport, and my clothes were all squirrelled away in my haversack and concealed in the loft where my parents never went.

I did think, many times, that I should speak to my parents and make an attempt to tell them how I was feeling. I needed to tell someone of the abuse and clear some of the horrors from my head into someone innocent. My 15-year-old guilty mind was telling me not to. It had all been my fault, they would hate me for what I had done, they would hate me for spurning my chance of stardom in this way, and so, I remained confined in myself.

I went off the rails quite a bit, unfortunately. I made some poor decisions over a short period of time. I had been arrested on four separate occasions on charges of theft, burglary, and criminal damage. Four wasn't a bad result, to be honest, should have been forty-four. After a few warnings and a couple of hours spent in a Police Cell, to see if I liked it, I was presented to Glasgow Sheriff Court. I was given three years' probation with a severe warning as to what would happen should I appear before the courts again. It didn't have the desired effect and very soon was missing appointments with my probation officer who then decided he would come to my home for the meetings. Often, I arranged to be somewhere else, much to his annoyance.

I had not made any firm plans, not made any final decisions, neither had I told a single person about my state of mind. It was going to be me and me alone who took the blame for anything and everything I was about to do. I was waiting until any evil thoughts began to smother me, and I was willing to act when they did. For now, I was ready.

It wasn't too long before my decision was made for me. I think it was a Saturday, early evening, and I was preparing to go out. I can't remember where or why and it's not important. I went into our lounge to tell mum I was going out. My father, sitting in his chair turned and told me if I was going anywhere near those 'fenian bastards' I wasn't to come back to his house. I took him literally. I didn't go near those 'fenian bastards' that night, but neither did I go back to his house. I quickly collected my concealment from the loft, walked out the front door and I was gone. The last words I heard were from mum telling me 'Not to be late'!

I knew the way; I'd been before with my guardian. Within 12 hours or so I was on the ferry from Dover to Calais. No-one recognised me and the cashier kept the till locked. It wouldn't have been a huge concern at first for my parents when they discovered my bed hadn't been slept in. It wasn't an unusual occurrence though this time my bed was to be empty for a very long time.

For probably 6 months or so I travelled through Europe. I had a total sense of freedom and was able to put many of the events that had tried to destroy me into captivity in the back of my mind.

Of course, I was incredibly short of cash and had many times been helped by those I met on the way. I had been able to get work on farms, sweeping garage forecourts, washing dishes in restaurants, and other career choices that didn't last long. My pocket was regularly topped up with other less acceptable methods. Shoplifting and selling on the booty was common-place, thefts from pockets within cloakrooms, and the removal of wallets and purses from unfortunate victims as they dined or drank in establishments throughout the continent. The occasional time spent begging in Railway Stations and other busy places was very often unproductive. Perhaps my age helped a little but the time it took to accrue what was needed to survive was lengthy and dangerous. I'm not proud of any of that in any way, in fact, totally ashamed of it all. I would far rather have avoided that aspect of my trip, but I had to eat, and this was a part of the solution. I apologise to every single person who was distressed, inconvenienced, or put into difficulty with my hurtful criminal actions whilst on-the-run.

At no time since I left home had I any thoughts of self-abuse. That element of my life had not been considered or felt necessary for a long time. I did though feel terrible pangs of guilt that I had left my mum under these circumstances. I was aware that she would be frantic at home with not knowing where I was or how I was. It was impossible to call her as I thought the call could be traced. I was also quite sure my disappearance would have been recorded with the police and I was no doubt a wanted man!

I hatched what I thought was a clever plan. I was in the north of Italy staying in a Youth Hostel and met a lively crowd of hitchhikers from Amsterdam. They were heading back to Holland the next day and they did me a massive favour. I quickly wrote a brief letter to mum. I can't remember the content but enough to let her know she was loved and that I was OK, I was free. I asked them to take the letter home with them to Holland and post it. When my mum received the letter from Holland, she would perhaps inform the authorities where I was, and all the time I would be in Italy or somewhere else. Certainly not Holland.

Of course, I was never certain if the letter was ever posted, as I was of others I wrote going forward. One was sent from Sweden when I was in Austria and a third from Italy when I was in Spain. When I did eventually return home, I discovered my mother had received them all. This eased the pain a little that I felt when she had told me on my return that she used to sit every night in my room, watching every number 67 bus from the city centre as it drew into the terminus across the road from our house. Praying, with her Rosary Beads, as every one of those thousands of buses arrived during my absence, that she would see me disembark and come home. I never did, not by bus anyway.

Portugal was where my respite adventure really took off in dramatic fashion. By this time, I had been away from home for roughly 6 months, probably longer, I had no interest in keeping track of time. I arrived in Lisbon and after meeting some fellow travellers, was advised that there were boats looking to increase their crew numbers down by the harbour. These guys had just left their own employ to head home. I had arrived in Lisbon without a Portuguese Escudo to my name. I was hungry and thirsty so headed down on foot to the harbour area. It was hot, too hot to have nothing to drink.

It wasn't long before I met up with a young crowd who were willing to point me in the right direction. I approached a few of the yachts berthed at the private marina who had signs stating their need for cabin crew. Within an hour I had secured a position with an American couple who were sailing with their baby daughter. They needed someone solely to do a night watch. To stay awake through the night as they slept as the yacht progressed on its proposed journey to Gibraltar, looking out for other vessels or anything else that posed a danger.

We sailed from Lisbon the following day after

having completed the immigration and customs checks at Lisbon immigration. At least I was now fed and watered and had the promise of $5 a day as recompense. It took a few nights to sail down the coast of Portugal and everything was going fairly well. I hadn't fallen asleep, and we hadn't hit anything on our course. Sines in Portugal was our intermediate stop as the couple wanted to take some supplies on board. I wasn't allowed to leave the yacht, something to do with immigration fees I remember being told. They dropped anchor a few hundred yards from shore and took the tender onto dry land.

They had decided to leave me with their baby ensuring me they would be back within the hour. That in itself did not pose any major issues. mum had been a foster-carer in my earlier years, and we often had new-born babies at home, for months at a time, until they were ready for their adoption. Changing nappies wasn't out with my realm and I was prepared, I thought. However, the baby had a catastrophic case of the shits, and I was changing nappies and cleaning up shit for the entire time they were away. When they eventually returned, long overdue, they were very apologetic. I hadn't signed up for that though and decided I had been with them long enough. I collected my due $20, and I was dropped off ashore to find my freedom again.

Within an hour on the quayside, I came across,

seriously, 'The Blue Peter'. A small French-owned yacht and they were also looking for crew members. The Parisian Captain was sailing down to the south of Portugal before heading across the Atlantic to the USA. The fact my passport already contained the required visa for the USA ensured I was taken on as a general crew member with another two Greek lads. He took my passport details and we set off the same night to Portimao, on the Algarve. Before we left, I posted a letter to my mother from Portugal. By the time she received it, I'd be in mid-Atlantic! She never did get that letter, the only letter I actually posted myself was, and still is, lost in the postal system, somewhere.

The 3-day trip was a nightmare. We were overworked and although we had agreed to a small payment of $100 when we arrived in the USA, we had been told our food and drink would be supplied. Food had been scarce, and our options were limited. We were only offered water to drink, nothing else. The three crew members were totally fucked off and were contemplating a mutiny, abandoning ship, and going our separate ways.

Once we were in Portimao the Parisian took a short walk from the boat over the sands, to shore (tide was well out) to go for a meal. He had left nothing for us to eat. The two Greeks went onto the sands to dig for crabs for our lunch and left me on the yacht alone. I'd had enough by this time and decided to go but not without my $100. I dropped down into the cabins area and forced the door open to enter his cabin. After a quick search, I found what I was looking for in a rather poorly secured wooden box under his bunk bed. I grabbed the lot. I had visions of throwing his passport to the fish but decided against it. The cash would be enough revenge as it was quite a wad. Transpired I had come into ownership of $2000 which at the exchange rate at the time was about £800. Today's equivalent in (2023) would be circa £15,000+. Some loose notes consisted of French Francs and Portuguese Escudos. I dumped half my clothes to make room for the cash in my haversack and I walked the sands following the captain's footsteps onto the shore and disappeared as fast as I could.

Of course, I knew I had to move quickly so I took a taxi into Lagos railway station and within an hour was on a train back to Lisbon. I was a very frightened young man but made the trip without an ounce of guilt or remorse. On arrival in Lisbon, early evening. I again took a taxi, this time to the airport. The first flight out of Lisbon was leaving in a couple of hours. It probably wouldn't have mattered where it was going. I just wanted out of Portugal before I was caught, returned to 'The Blue Peter', and forced to walk the plank 1000 miles from anywhere. The flight was an air Alitalia on its way to New York City. I showed my passport, bought my ticket ($250,

£100, the exchange rate at the time was $2.5 to the £1), and prepared to board quickly.

An hour or so before the flight was due to depart, I started through immigration to the boarding area. Crash... I was asked to stand to one side and a senior immigration official beckoned me to follow him into a room for questioning. It transpired that when I left Lisbon with the Americans my passport had been stamped with a Portuguese exit stamp. As I had not gone through immigration again after my stint on 'The Blue Peter', I had an exit but no re-entry stamp. They were quite curious as to why. I explained to them that I had changed my mind and left the yacht before it had even left Lisbon and couldn't understand why my Passport had not been stamped on re-entry. I was terrified they would search my haversack and was desperately trying to think of anything that would justify my enviable wealth. It was Customs fault, I had presented it, but they had obviously, simply omitted to stamp it! Fortunately, they called on an Alitalia representative to assist and after a half-hour or so they consented and let me proceed.

I was shaking uncontrollably until I had boarded, and the flight took off for the Land of the Free. Once in the air I relaxed, smiled, and slept like a baby, a baby with no shits and no Torbett anywhere. From that day to today I have never set foot again in Portugal. I always had visions of being taken to the side in immigration and asked if I had been in Portimao in 1970?

Another problem arose at JFK Airport when an immigration officer asked me where my luggage was. Having just a small haversack I had aroused suspicion. True to form my quick thinking explained that my parents had sent my luggage on in advance to a family member, so I didn't have to carry it. With an eventual acceptance of my explanation, he checked my visa again and waved me through, and I had arrived in America.

Another taxi ride saw me in New York City. I was dropped off at a Greyhound bus terminal. I had no plans, but I was tired after the flight and wanted something to eat and a cold drink. Pepsi and burger were on my agenda, so I ordered and waited for the staff to bring it over to my table at the window.

I sat thinking of mum, hoping she would get my letter soon. I should have made a telephone call to her from Lisbon airport considering I was just about to fly out of Portugal anyway. She hadn't heard my voice, nor me hers, for such a long time and I knew her heart would be breaking to hear it and to know I was safe. I didn't though and it would be many months before she heard from me again. That saddened me, but I had to shrug it off quickly and dismiss my guilt. My meal arrived, I was ravenous and destroyed it quickly.

As I relaxed, I was joined by a couple of young lads who asked who, why and, where questions that left me uneasy. They suggested I come over to meet their boss who was looking for young lads to come and work for him. I declined and started to get ready to make a move. The gentleman in question moved over and sat at my table. He asked if I was looking for a job? I'm quite sure my previous experiences had made me sufficiently suspicious of 'these people' and felt I could see them coming from a distance. I was beginning to think Torbett had perhaps branded me with something that indicated I was easy prey. I told him I was interested but would first have to go and meet a friend who was arriving by coach. I left with a promise to be back within the hour and on looking up at the departures I quickly booked a Greyhound Ticket to the first available destination.

A few minutes later I was aboard my coach preparing to depart for Montreal. To this day I am quite sure at that moment in New York I was in grave danger. I'm convinced he was a pimp, and he was recruiting youngsters to have their lives shattered. I had learned to my cost that paedophiles can easily recognise a run-away or a child in distress, they pounce. My life had already been shattered so I was most certainly on the defensive, it saved me that day. I left New York shortly afterward and even today have bad feelings about that city.

Over the next 6 weeks or so I travelled across Canada eventually to arrive in Vancouver. On the way, I met many characters of varying ages and positions in life. From the young and beautiful Vikki Zaremba in Toronto with whom I stayed for a few days to the junkies I spent time with within youth hostels and cheap hotels. They were happy with their weed and their intravenous addictions, something I witnessed many times but never took part, neither did anyone try to coerce me to do so. Despite their obvious shortcomings and desperation for cash, I never felt threatened, was never attacked, never an attempt to rob me, or cause me harm. The Canadians were a joy to be with regardless of their own personal misfortunes and standings in life. I did however spend a great deal of my own, hard-stolen money in assisting them with the necessities but not, once, did I pay for their drugs.

I left Canada via another Greyhound and re-entered America. I put my New York experience down to a one-off and decided to give the USA another opportunity to impress me. Via Pace Arch, I entered Washington State. Over the next few days, I travelled through Oregon into California. After a stop off in San Francisco, I continued to Los Angeles. Santa Monica was where I was heading as I had a contact there who I hadn't seen for a year or more. Bill Rock, chairman of the Los Angeles Celtic Supporters Association, whom I had met once at a dinner at

Celtic Park. He was a resident of Santa Monica. I remember, at that meeting, him showing me a photograph of his impressive car, not as impressive as Big Jocks but hugely impressive none-the-less. It had the Californian registration plate 'CELTIC'.

On arrival in Santa Monica, I had a good look around and went into a restaurant that had caught my attention. 'Old Mahoney's Irish Whip'. I ordered a meal and a drink and asked if they knew of a Bill Rock. Surprisingly, they did. A call was put into Bill, and he called back from his place of work at Los Angeles Airport.

Arrangements were made to meet up the next day and for that evening I spent the night on the sofa of the Irish barmaid and her American husband. To this day I can remember Bill's address in Santa Monica. The street number too but it's not important.

Bill and I met up the next day and of course he was astonished to see me. He welcomed me into his home, and I spent a week or so there with his family before we had a heart-to-heart talk one night and I told him I was a run-away. He had suspected that of course and we decided on a course of action that would see me return to my family. I agreed to go home on the condition he did not contact Celtic Football Club, nor indeed my parents. I did not feel the need to burden him with my Torbett experience and had insisted family problems had been my reason to travel. He arranged a ticket for me to fly home the following Saturday which I was unable to pay for. Working as he did at the airport; he did however get me a vastly discounted flight and the cost from Los Angles via Boston to Prestwick was $120 dollars. I was told later that he had contacted Celtic Football Club and that they had forwarded the money to get me back to the UK, no evidence of that unfortunately.

I arrived at Prestwick and took the train into Glasgow. It was so strange being back in my city again and mostly, thankfully, the memories were respectful. I was on a train again to Muirend within a few minutes and at 9.30 a.m. on Monday morning I rang our front doorbell for the first time in over a year.

I was unsure whether or not to hide and tease mum a little more, but my new grown-up persona told me not to. Mum opened the door and cried. I did too!

Why may you think was this chapter necessary? It highlights how my abuse at Celtic's Boys' Club forced me into this journey. If I had not met Keith that sunny Saturday morning I would still have been at home, taking my mum's side with all things sectarian. I would have been safe, whole, not shattered, and there is every likelihood I would have been a happy young man who had grown from a normal child with only the memories and dreams a child should have?

My trip had most certainly allowed me to cast away many of the things that had originally compelled me to go. It gave me an opportunity to start afresh, to a point, and prepare for the rest of my life positively.

That was the plan and to a degree, it would prove to be partly successful though, the memories of the abuse would encroach every so often and ensure total erasure of my turmoil would be impossible.

15. BORSTAL AVOIDED

I had not seen my probation officer for over a year, so I contacted him a few weeks after my return and was concerned at what he had to say on the telephone. He wasn't happy of course and arranged to call at my home the following day to discuss my absenteeism with him.

On arrival, he wasted no time in advising me it was already out of his hands and had been passed back to the Courts as a breach of probation. He could do nothing to help me now and advised me to pop into the local Police station and refer them to the warrant that had been issued for my immediate arrest many months prior. I was sixteen by this time and didn't expect to be given any allowances for my young age. That had been a lifeline already offered to me with the original sentence and I was well aware of how serious a breach of probation was in the eyes of the justice system at the time.

It was the following day when my mum and sister accompanied me down to the local police station and made them aware of who I was and why I was reporting. We were taken to a side room where a few telephone calls were made to determine the facts. I fully expected to be detained to appear in Court the next day. Surprisingly they were unable to locate the warrant and was advised to go home and await a visit once they had located the paperwork needed to expedite an arrest. The next day we were visited by a Sergeant who explained I would receive a summons to appear and that no arrest was necessary in consideration my family had assured them I would not abscond again, and they would ensure my appearance… not a wise decision!

I was a little bastard in the intervening period and made everyone's life a misery at home. My time away had given me the confidence to speak up for myself although many times that conviction was overspent and culminated in me abusing anyone who stood in my way.

The summons arrived and I prepared to face my executioner. I felt this was an opportunity to perhaps explain to the authorities what had happened and why I was taking this particularly unpleasant path in life. The date came and we left early to go to Glasgow Sheriff Court. Again, my mum and sister were there for what I had assumed was support and welcomed their attendance. As I prepared what I was going to say I decided this was not the time to release the dark information that I had been concealing. Primarily because I knew I would not be believed but also that the total shame of my behaviour was still uppermost in my mind. The guilt I was feeling was still so severe that admitting my actions to the Sheriff would probably get me jailed for longer.

I had been told by my eldest brother to pray I wasn't called before Sheriff Middleton as he had a reputation of coming down hard on young delinquents. My brother had prior knowledge.

My name was called mid-morning and I was ushered into the courtroom and went directly to the dock. The Judge entered and took his seat. I had an urge to smirk at the wig but managed to contain my stupidity until the need passed. I leaned over to my court-appointed lawyers and asked him who the judge was. Sheriff Middleton was the reply.

Oh well, thanks to my brother I had a lot less hope and was now a lot more apprehensive, and fearful than I would have been if only he had kept his mouth shut. He had expanded at the time by giving me examples of the sentences Middleton had dished out for relatively minor offences committed by members of The Drumchapel 'Buck'. A gang of youths, in their thousands, who scoured the area for years causing havoc. Two of my three brothers had been members and were well known to the Courts, my brother 'Andy', was the 'Leader Off'.

Middleton heard from the probation service, and they put their case strongly against me. I had missed more than 80% of my appointed meetings with the officer attached to my case. My lawyer tried his best to mitigate on my behalf, but it certainly didn't compare favourably with the case against me. Middleton then asked my mother and my sister in turn to give their opinions as to what options were available as a family unit that may be instrumental in swaying his sentencing one way or another. To my utter disbelief both of those I trusted turned and made the most damning statement against me. They had both testified that I was out of control and that they were unable to handle my behaviour both in and outwith the home. Any authority they tried to implement was disregarded and only forced me to rebel even more. They both said the only option they could see that would perhaps be effective for them to regain their control and set me on a pathway to compliance would be a custodial sentence.

My heart dropped like a brick. There was no coming back from that and nothing I could say would dissuade the Sheriff from passing another stern custodial sentence which would have meant a borstal term.

I was now allowed to speak. My own family's treachery had left me emotional, tearful, and unable to put my defence, even if I had had one, across coherently. I spoke about my trip away and what had made me go citing nothing other than my great sadness at home and the disappointment I had faced due to my Celtic failure. I apologised and assured the Sheriff; I had convinced myself whilst away that I needed to conform and fully intended to do so.

I had done all I could and as instructed sat down, barely able to see the Judge over the docks brass bar. The judge read through some papers, and he then over-ruled his own previous instruction and told me to stand. I wasn't sure if my legs would be able to keep me upright or if they would remain strong enough to take me down the stairs to the cells.

Many things, as I've said before, are a bit unclear to me. One thing though, I can remember Sheriff Middleton's statement, near enough word for word. I'll never forget them.

"Young man, you have the makings of a very good conman, a professional thief, and a stain on our society. You are already a stain on the name of your good family. I have listened to the prosecution, and I have listened to your defence. More importantly, I have listened to your family, and they are quite confident that custody is the only answer to our problem here. What do I do?

My immediate thoughts are of a 12-month custodial sentence. However, though I cannot put my finger on it, I see something in you, and this whole situation concerns me. I see some good and I don't want to destroy that. Gordon, you are being given one last chance. I am going to extend your probation period for 24 months. In that time, should you miss one appointment, be involved in one more element of crime of any description, I will ensure you appear in front of me, and should that happen, you will be a very sorry young man, I promise you. You are free to go and make arrangements with your probation officer outside the Courtroom before you leave.

He punched the gavel down, stood and left the Courtroom as I turned tearfully, hugged my mum and sister, and said how sorry I was to them both. I meant it. Fortunately, from that day to this I have respected the chance I was given by upholding his belief in me. Well, other than one unfortunate mistake eight years later when I made a wrong choice, was found out and paid the price for my stupidity.

On weighing up what had happened that day I lay in bed thankful for the opportunity to avoid borstal. I'm sure it would have broken me further and would surely have made any comeback to normality impossible. I vowed I was going to change and sort myself out. I had made vows before, unsuccessfully, this time I was going to succeed. One thing that was foremost in my mind was that without Torbett, none of this would have happened. I was still allowing the bastard to control my thoughts and my deeds. I was allowing him to continue to destroy any future I had, and I knew I had to put a stop to that before it was too late, far too late! I won most of that battle.

It wasn't long after that I decided I couldn't stay in the family home and at just 16 years old I moved into a room within a shared flat in Shawlands and never returned home.

I'm not sure if the strain of everything had this effect or if their relationship was going down that path anyway but it wasn't long before mum and dad separated and then divorced after thirty-odd years of marriage. My dad stayed in the matrimonial home and my mum moved to be near family and friends in Ipswich. I never did find out if my experiences and actions had contributed to the marriage breakdown, I never asked.

From then on, my visits to either were very few and far between. Years would pass with no contact, I felt at the time that was what was best for me.

I decided to write to Sheriff Middleton to thank him for his decision and how I had responded to his trust in me mid 1980s. A few weeks later I received a letter of reply from someone advising me he had passed away a short time before. They had, hopefully, passed my letter onto his family. I never heard from them, but I earnestly hope it gave them some pride and deserved respect for their amazing father who was able to see behind a child's eyes when that child needed it most.

16. THE YEARS BETWEEN

My life through the years between Celtic Boys' Club and coming forward were uneventful in relation to my overall story. Of course, my experiences throughout did haunt me at times, but I always had the strength, mostly, to put them to one side and to continue with the aims that I had placed before me.

I settled and became a solid citizen and was content with my lot.

I fell in love, married, and had two wonderful children in those days. I had a successful career and was proud of many of my achievements including winning monthly top UK salesman, 79 times out of 84, with one of the organisations I worked with when I had over 100+ salesman competitors. I set up my own business in 1986 which was very successful for a long-time employing 30+ employees and is still going today albeit trimmed down after retirement to just me doing what I love to do.

Financially I was OK, bought a home for the family, had nice holidays abroad with them and the children went for nothing.

Now and again, sadly, that existence, that survival would be interrupted and leave me distressed, feeling alone and desperate and unable to cope. Those interruptions were most certainly the responsibility of the evil Jim Torbett and the involvement of the Celtic organisation and the Celtic Family in my young life.

There were then and still are today elements of those days, that abuse, that will never leave me. They deserve to be cast from my conscious into the firepit of Hell, they are, often, but some bastard keeps throwing them back out at me.

There was one aspect that I could never quite come to terms with and that was offering my unconditional attention and love to my children. Only as they grew up and became more dependent on attention, love, and physical contact did it become clear to me I was not the person who could give them that. I was terrified of being close to them physically, unable to touch them, kiss them and care for them as every other parent finds part and parcel of being a good parent. Simply put, I could not cope with being a father. That longed for element in my life had been given to me and I was unable to do what I was required to do. Not because I didn't want to, I was desperate to change but I failed. I failed to change, I failed my children, and I failed as a father, and I had failed my wife as a husband. Time to move on sadly.

I had the very uncomfortable conversations with my wife, and we separated. On several occasions I made a huge effort, and we got back together, tried again but my demons would return, and it was proven time and time again I wasn't going to be able to stay with my family.

My ex-wife was never confided in as to what was causing my obvious want to move on without them. She found out 35 years later along with everyone else when my story broke in the Daily Record on 28th October 2019. A few days before my sons 44th birthday. I had confided in my oldest daughter a few days before and told her everything and that the story was about to break. Her initial response was "it explains a lot dad", that hurt, and one day I may even ask her what she meant by that. She was 7 when I left the family home and now, 35 years later, she was being given a part of the reasons why she lost her dad.

Don't get me wrong, I kept in touch and saw the two children regularly. I made frequent telephone calls to them as well as visits both ways and was always there for them for any problems they had growing up but that was not enough and I'm aware deep down they resented me leaving. I know and I accept that. Sadly, there is nothing I can do to right those wrongs and nothing I can do to give those children back the part of their childhood they lost.

I am not alone, how many children, how many wives, how many parental delights have been lost because of those bastards and what they did to little boys, children for over 30+ years?

How many of those little boys have had to go through what I went through? It makes me cry!

Fuck every last one of them, sadistic perpetrators and their evil enablers who have only an eternity in Hell to look forward to. As each of you die, I'll raise a glass to your rightful custodian.

17. FLASHBACKS

Coercive control is partly a pattern or acts of sexual assault, threats, humiliation, punishment & intimidation, or other abuse that is used to harm or frighten a child, forcing compliance. This is mostly adult-related but can easily be associated with what happens to abused children. Think about experiencing that as a child and that may come some way in explaining why the flashbacks have such an enormous impact!

To have your sexual virginity stolen from you in such a savage way is barred from any escape. It cannot be regained, and it cannot be replaced with anything other than haunting memories. How many times is an individual asked throughout their lifetime when they lost their virginity. To many, the question is loaded and intended to be in jest, a question that in the grand scale of life is not an important issue and of course many people lie to save their embarrassment. However, to a victim who has had that stolen from them, all that the jesting introduces is horror, memories, and a desperate need to forget, you're so often not allowed to.

Despite the debilitating, continuing, flashbacks, now infrequent but still a part of me I'm afraid, I've opened up too many, perhaps millions, and hopefully my words will demonstrate how hard that has been. But believe me, every tear I've shed since I came forward has been in honour of those who can't, whether that be through misplaced shame, guilt, fear of not being believed, or the many who have passed before they could muster their courage to do so, I honour them and their memory.

Flashbacks are painful, frightening, distressing, and can set the victim back ten steps for every one they've bravely taken. It's widely thought they occur as a victim sleeps. That's partly true but the flashbacks take all guises and can be mild or severe, can happen and be triggered at any time, in a vast range of circumstances. Some can be avoided though many cannot, and the victim must try to cope with these as best they can. How they affect the individual is also outwith their control and may be relative to other problems being faced at that time.

As I said before, it's a near on impossibility for a victim to avoid the triggers of flashbacks. They can happen when innocently watching TV and suddenly, without warning, there is a report. A new signing, a player being transferred, an upcoming fixture, results of a past fixture, any news about the club is televised and thrown at the victim without his permission on a regular basis and that brings the memories rushing back into unprepared minds. Newspaper articles are constant, everywhere you go there will inevitably be someone wearing the hoops of Celtic proudly, it's their club so why shouldn't they? All these daily reminders inflict memories on victims that they are desperate to avoid.

What I could never get my head around is that despite the growing number of allegations, criminal convictions, and publicity surrounding the scandal at that organisation there did not seem to be any appetite to be disgusted, at the very least, by what had already been made public about the goings-on within the Celtic family. Moral repugnance was absent in its entirety. Board members went about their daily business lacking any interest or care, high-profile, famous, public figures showered the club with their support and at times, sickening devotion. I was always amazed to see football managers come and go, star players signing for the club, major, famous international companies sponsoring the club for countless millions all without, apparently, any interest in what was now becoming very evident, that a paedophile ring had been and possibly still was, operating within that very same Celtic family when they signed the dotted line to pay them millions. Some, though not too many, were being reported on television and in newspapers, which gave the victims of sickening abuse no respite. All these points were instrumental in introducing flashbacks into the nightmares and daily lives of surviving victims and often they trespassed with a vengeance.

Depending on the mindset of the victim at the

point of being assaulted by flashbacks would dictate their severity. At times it can be shrugged off with a concerted effort into filling your mind with something positive. Other times the victim is not quite so lucky, and the intrusion will dictate to them how the rest of their day, week, or month will unfold. Many a time I've been looking forward to a day at the beach, a visit to the cinema, a meal at a restaurant, or 1001 other things that I have had to abort and feign illness, tiredness, or some other just as ridiculous reason for going home, disappointing myself and whoever just happened to be with me was a frequent event and one that was unavoidable.

Of course, the nightmare flashbacks were much worse. Desperate to waken from them as they were often so realistic and ensured the victim had to relive the abuse over and over again. On awakening, you feel no real sense of relief at having the nightmare stop but rather an overwhelming feeling of distress, regret, and a continuance of the guilt you felt as a child. It could be days, or in severe cases months, before your thought pattern would return to a normal peaceful existence.

Until the next time.

18. MUM & DAD PASS

I had not seen mum, I don't think, for near on 6 years. My father probably even longer. I had distanced myself as best as I could from as many memories as I could. I blamed no-one, of course, other than myself, Celtic Football Club and Torbett. I at no time blamed any of my family. The decisions I had made all those years ago had been mine and mine alone. My only real regret over those decisions was that I had not listened to my father. I had not followed the herd. I had convinced myself by that time that my father and my brothers had been right all along in so many of their beliefs. I should have taken note and not been a 'bambi".

These paedophile animals just don't realise the damage they do or maybe they do but their own sadistic sexual needs outstrip everything else. Not just to the young lives they trespass, into, uninvited, but also the damage they inflict on the adults who morph from those same, sorry children. As they grow the children still have to live with the guilt, the horrific memories, the need to distance themselves from family and friends which in turn is a tragedy for those families and friends who silently accept they have lost someone from their lives for no apparent reason?

Those who progress to having their own families are still locked up in their views of adult, child relationships. I can remember feeling very guilty if I hugged my son or my daughters, whether as a toddler, a pre-teen, or a teen. When I sat them on my knee, I always felt uncomfortable. I was unable to give my own children the physical contact their peers, fortunately, were able to enjoy from their own parents. Can you imagine your child desperate for a cuddle from their dad only to be turned away and how that must have made them feel? That's what I went through. Can you imagine your child hurting themselves in a fall or having emotional problems and not having a reassuring hug from their dad? That's what they went through!

It wasn't me who refused to love my children the way I should have, it was Celtic Boys' Club and Torbett who did that to my innocent kids. The paedophiles, and their enablers, were also guilty of my off-springs abuse too. In fact, anyone who came into my life after that terrible time was probably affected in some way by that abuse!

Many of those tragic individuals have plummeted into alcoholism, drug addiction, crime, self-abuse, and worst of all suicide. This leads to the loss of beautiful young people, in their prime, with so much to give to their families, friends, and most importantly, to themselves.

The nightmares the victims have to live with until the day they die are bloodcurdlingly horrific. Compare that to the relative ease in which paedophiles can handle their own deserved nightmares, of one day being exposed, convicted, and dealt with by a repulsed public. There is absolutely no justifiable comparison, none whatsoever!

I can't remember who made the call advising me of my mum's ill-health. I do remember feeling ashamed that I hadn't been in touch for so long. I was given her telephone number in Brightlingsea, Essex that I didn't have, and prepared myself to make a telephone call to her to offer my support and love. Long-time overdue. I knew it wasn't going to be an easy call. I also know it was going to be much worse for mum than it would for me. I know my absence from her life recently would have had an effect on her life to a far greater negative degree than mine. Little did I realise though that she had had her own suspicions for my lack of contact over the years and she was spot on. We would discuss that in the months to come.

Mum had been diagnosed with cancer and had been told that she had about 3 months before that relentless disease would take her from her loved ones. As my mum answered my call her surprise went unrecorded. We didn't speak long, and I arrange to travel down from Manchester, where I had a branch office, and living at the time, to see her at her home.

It was a sad day when I finally got to see her.

We attempted to disguise the many years we had been apart, but it wasn't easy. It was early summer, I think, and mum's only concern was that she could see one more Christmas. She loved Christmas and always tried to make it so special for everyone. In fact, one year she arranged for Santa to bring me a 'Mouldmaster' ball, yes that one. Other Christmas gifts had always been shared between all the children, but the ball was mine. I know I've mentioned that before, but I make no apology for mentioning it again.

Time went on and mum fought as we all knew she would. Thankfully, she saw another Christmas much to the amazement of her doctors. Through her physical treatment and her mental disorientation, mum was passing the short time she had left playing Scrabble with the family, when they visited which was often.

After Christmas, I visited early in the New Year. She only asked me for one thing... to see one more Christmas. Her illness was grabbing hold and time for everyone was marching on slowly except hers, mums time was progressively passing faster, and speeding at a rate that distressed her. I took time from work and decided to move to Brightlingsea temporarily to help all I could. One of my brothers lived in Brightlingsea and he and his wife had been looking after mum throughout her illness. Whereas I was careful not to interfere with that I wanted to offer any support to mum that I could. After dinner one evening we were watching T.V., and mum asked me to turn it down as she wanted to talk. I expected the same old "I just want to see one more Christmas...", an offering my mum would ensure we were aware of daily. As the T.V. silenced she asked me if I had heard about Jim Torbett. I hadn't and I told her so. She then went on to tell me Torbett had recently been jailed for two years for abusing 3 of the kids and that the timing of the abuse coincided with the time I was at the club. She asked if anything had ever happened to me and I lied to her, again. My mother was ill, frail, her days were being drawn down and there was no way I was going to allow anything to bring her down any faster. There was not a chance in hell I was going to inflict my painful memories on my mother at this stage. I knew she desperately wanted to know, and I desperately wanted her not to. So, I lied over and over again and hoped that was the end of it. I had, through choice, decided to avoid any hurt to my family, any blame to be attributed to them, any guilt they may have felt necessary to take on board, by keeping my secret and adopting a non-disclosure approach. It was important to me to protect them all, especially mum.

There was silence for a while and she then announced: "Gordon, your dad and I found a letter you wrote to Jim Torbett asking him to stop hurting you". Mum explained that my dad had sent my letter with a covering letter of complaint to Jock Stein at Celtic Park. My mother said that he got no response.

On hearing this news from my dying Mother, a part of my jigsaw locked together. The night when Torbett had been, unexpectedly, invited into our home for a coffee, the raised voices would indicate my father had approached and questioned him about the letter I had written to him. Within a week or so of my father's letter to Celtic, I was thrown out of Celtic's Boys' Club, and it is my firm belief Jock Stein was behind that decision which Torbett, perhaps reluctantly, enforced. I was saddened at the time, but at last, I was safe.

By this point, as I said, I had kept my silence for over 30 years. I had been desperate to protect my parents, my family, and my friends, from having to be affected by the abuse. One victim in the family was clearly enough. The thought that each and every day of those 30 years had been in vain and that they too had shared my secret, silently, distressed me greatly and was the first stage to me being hospitalised shortly afterwards.

You may ask, as many have done over these years fighting for the justice we so richly deserve, why my father allowed me to return to the Boys' Club albeit only for a very short time and why he didn't phone the police? I think when you consider the history of my father and my relationship, he did not want it to appear to me that he was responsible for me losing my place within the Celtic family. He left it to Celtic to do that and they did so, abruptly, and effectively, except they didn't phone the police either, despite it being their duty to do so. They removed the victim but willingly kept the perpetrator!

Mum's revelation ensured I was trapped, nowhere to go other than to ask my mum to leave it be and talk about something else. She respected my wishes now and nodded in agreement. Mum closed the conversation by saying "Just be careful Gordon, if you open a can of worms, you had better be prepared to eat them." I think we could see the pain in each other's eyes and no more was said. What else either of those letters contained, when it was written or why it was written, I can't remember, I'll never know, to be honest, I didn't want to know then and I don't want to know now.

One thing that did hit me at that time and hit me hard was that if Torbetts' depravity had been addressed at that point there is a good chance none of the subsequent abuse would have happened at Celtic. The hundreds upon hundreds of young lives devastated could have been avoided if only Mr Stein had read my dad's letter and called the police. There might not have been any more Torbett victims, there may not have been any McCafferty, Cairney, King, Cullen, Brown, Strachan, McCauley, or Divers' victims. Of course, it may be that they were not all directly employed by Celtic when the abuse took place but as far as I'm concerned, they all learned their 'paedophilic expertise' in the 'Celtic School of paedophilia'.

I've only mentioned here the convicted Celtic associated paedophiles. There are probably more and of course Malley only escaped his impending charges and trial due to his death! It is on record that Police were given the names of 14 men who needed to be investigated.

Torbett had, I've no doubt, been instrumental in his other, now convicted paedophile friends, being offered positions with the Celtic's Boys' Club. They were all animals from the same cage, if Torbett had been removed in 1968, the others may never have been a part of the 'Celtic Family'. Other children from other organisations would still have been abused by these people because they would all have sourced the children for their disgusting needs elsewhere. It just might not have happened at Celtic Football Club.

After a few minutes, my mum got up and declared that she had something for me. I feared she had the letter and was not about to let it drop. When she returned, she silently handed me a package, I opened it and I burst into tears. The package contained the plaque I had been awarded for the St Benedicts Cup Final at Parkhead 30 years prior. When I had left the family home on my world tour my father had ensured all my Celtic memorabilia, newspaper clippings, photographs, strips, medals, uniform, my cherished Mouldmaster, trophies, and apparently letters, were destroyed, binned, or set alight and my mother had retrieved this one item, she had kept it safe for 30 years. I could say nothing other than "Thank you". But I still lied about everything else.

It was now late November; mum's cancer took a grip, and she was admitted to St Helena Hospice in Colchester. She had been there many times for respite during the times the family needed support. She was looked after amazingly by Nurse Laney. Mum took to her, as we all did, and her comfort in her final days was attributed greatly to her dedication.

The doctor at the hospital gave mum a sedative after explaining to her that she would fall asleep, be pain-free, and eventually pass without waking up. It was mum's choice to take the sedative as the alternative was not an option. We had been told it would take a few hours for the sedative to force her final sleep. She dropped off into a light sleep, though not sedative related, just an every-day afternoon nap, and rested. My brother and I quickly found the Hospice's Christmas decorations. We silently decorated her room, a tree, fairy lights and, Christmas music on the player. We arranged for family, staff, and other residents to pay mum a visit or call to wish her a Merry Christmas. Mum had seen one more Christmas!

Doctors had told us they were unsure if patients could hear whilst under their final sedative. We were advised to talk to mum as much as possible. In the event she could hear us she would know she was not alone. We spoke to her constantly.

Mum slept for 2 full days before cancer took her. I sat at her bedside as my brother also did, often taking turns, as my mum had asked us to make sure she wasn't alone. During that time, we held her hand constantly and re-assured her. I had a tremendous urge to confess everything to mum as she slept. I wanted to off-load but I couldn't bring myself to do it. I cried for my mother, and I cried for myself. I had an opportunity now after 30 years to confide and to free myself from some of the abhorrent memories I had shared only with my own nightmares. I thought, how could I be so selfish to even consider loading my dying mother with this. I fought the urge for two days before, when we were alone, I simply said to mum, as she slept, that she had nothing to blame herself for with regards to my time at Celtic, I did not elaborate. I felt her hand grip mine ever so gently. I pray to any and all Gods to assure me that she heard.

Nurse Laney was intimately attending to mum, so we had to leave the room momentarily. After a few minutes, she came into the visitors' room and told my brother and me to return quickly as mum was going very fast. My brother held her as I stroked her shoulders to let her know she was not alone. Mum only breathed for a few minutes more. She passed.

I took stock of everything and couldn't convince myself that I had 'done the right thing'. It was then that I decided on my return home I was going to see my father and intended to tell him everything. Open my heart to him when at the same time assuring him that he should also be guilt-free. It was important that my family should not be abused by Torbett in any way shape or form. It was important that I tell them it was me and those evil bastards, perpetrators, and enablers but certainly not my family, not them. My mother had spent valuable minutes before her death thinking about Torbett and my abuse when she should have had happy family memories to fill those last moments in her life. For that James Torbett, I despise you.

I also wanted to ask my dad about the conversation I had had with mum before she passed. I needed clarity about when he had found the letter, I had written to Torbett, when he had written to Celtic and how long after that had I been dismissed from any further participation with Celtic's Boys' Club. I had my own ideas of course but to have those confirmed was now very important to me to allow me to go forward and put to death, even if only some of the confusion that had been haunting me for so long. I was determined to get this meeting with dad over and done with as soon as possible with the intention of hopefully freeing us both from some of the mental horrors that had prevailed for 30 years and more after they had been introduced into my innocent life. Unfortunately, an unexpected twist of fate was to destroy any chance of this, late-in-the-day release.

We were, as a family, preparing to say goodbye to mum for the last time. Sue Laney had invited me over to her house for dinner as we had become quite close during the time I spent at the hospice. After we had eaten, we sat, talking about mum, and going over all the good memories I had of her. I tried to avoid many memories of course but they always seemed to find a way to creep in.

A telephone call came in and it was for me, from my brother. My father had taken a massive stroke in Scotland and had been admitted to Crosshouse Hospital in Kilmarnock, Ayrshire. We were advised to get there as soon as possible as the situation was not good.

My brother and I left immediately to drive from Brightlingsea to Kilmarnock. We arrived at the hospital to find our father in a coma. For several days other members of the family congregated around his bedside to will him on and to let him know we were all there. My father never regained consciousness. He passed.

I had been unable to speak to him. I really don't know what upset me more. His passing or my inability to remove from his conscience any trace of guilt he may have had.

Neither mum nor dad had really seen one more Christmas and had passed within weeks of each other. Hopefully, they were celebrating Christmas together somewhere else and both with the knowledge that Protestant or Catholic, it didn't matter, there would be no more 'fenian bitch' nor 'orange bastard', they would be friends! That same filthy bastard who had abused me so many years ago was still doing so. 30 years had passed, and he was still controlling my thoughts, my guilts, my family, and my love for my parents.

Despite everything that had transpired during my childhood, I still loved them both dearly, despite my absences. Now they were gone, I was so, sorry!

These events destroyed me for some time. A few months after their passing I was just not coping, and my own sinister thoughts were taking over me completely. I desperately needed to talk to them both and to correct my lies and my silence that I had been guilty of for 30 years. I could only do that if I was with them. I found myself seeking methods and alternatives to end my own life. Of course, I had many options but to my fragile mind, this was the best one and the only one that I had full control over. I was sick and tired of being controlled by my memories, I needed to take the control that would best serve my cause.

My children intervened within my own mind, and I eventually sought the help of my family doctor in Stewarton, who had me admitted to a mental health unit, within hours, where I stayed for some time. On my eventual release, I am glad to say those feelings had gone and have never returned. When I decided to come forward and to subsequently write my book, I did have a fear they could return and perhaps this time the outcome may not be as successful. I have, as best I can, monitored my own mental health throughout the past few years' progress and can be confident those demons have been laid to rest, never to reappear.

I am thankful for that as it's important for me to finish this journey on behalf of every single victim, of the Celtic Boys' Club and every single child abused at the hands of animals everywhere. Perhaps there are those that would rather I did not speak on their behalf, in those cases I guarantee I'm not, only for the silent ones and victims who are no longer with us and who have passed without speaking out, I would like to think I speak for them too.

That journey still has a little way to go. Once all those brave men involved in the upcoming class-action lawsuit against Celtic achieve their justice and can get on with their lives knowing their perpetrator and his enabler have answered to a Court of Law, will I be satisfied, and I can happily hang up my boots.

19. THE RIGHT THING TO DO

I had thought, many times over the decades, to make my story known, each time I convinced myself not to. The relief I could possibly achieve by doing so was always beaten well into second place by the fear of the fall-out. The expected denials from the perpetrators themselves and the difficulty of the road ahead due to the many deniers and non-believers. They could, and most certainly would make my life a living hell all over again. It would, rather than allow me to come to terms with everything, dispel my guilt and accept my innocence, throw me into an even heavier turmoil than before and possibly re-introduce my guilt with a vengeance and I knew I was not strong enough to handle all that, any of that.

Of course, that is exactly how the groomers, and the paedophiles want you to feel. It is their modus-operandi. This was not a strategy developed by the evil beast Torbett himself. This was understood to be the safest way to avoid capture throughout their world. A world very much connected with each other's paedophile rings and groups of paedophiles being involved and helping each other, comparing notes, and teaching each other how to be invisible and successful in their depravity. They ensured the guilt always lay with the victim, made them ashamed of what they had done, and eliminate any thoughts they may have of seeking help because it was forced onto the child what the consequences would be if they dared to open their innocent little mouths. They knew then and still do today that they were sentencing these children to a lifetime of self-loathing.

When I did come forward and decided to write my story, I discovered a problem. There are many things that caused me some confusion when I started to put my experiences onto paper, both for the book and the police statement. I have difficulty putting events in the order they occurred. I have written as I recall the incidents and not necessarily exactly when they happened. It is important to remember, and I thank you for understanding, that the events mentioned in the writing are only the attacks and other events I remember clearly having actually taken place. There were many other incidents of abuse that I cannot recall clearly enough to commit to paper. Some I have deliberately erased from my memory for eternity. How bad they were I cannot tell you but bad enough that my sub-conscious, my self-preservation instinct, and other psychological issues may make them impossible to recall. I cannot in all honesty force a recall for you as that is when they become tainted, they can manifest as a figment of imagination rather than a reality and for that reason they are better left where they are, for now.

Initially, each time I thought of approaching the

police, the press, or the lawyers, the thoughts passed, and I reverted into my comfortable silent world. I tried, over the years, to avoid any mention of The Celtic's Boys' Club abuse scandal so I was not reminded, but of course the relentless coverage in the media and TV reports made that difficult. Not just the abuse reports, every time a family member wanted to watch a Celtic game on T.V., I was reminded. Every single mention of Celtic, their successes, and their failures was a reminder. Just seeing an innocent passer-by in the street wearing the hoops was a reminder.

My heart went out to every case I heard about over the years. The first being my conversation with mum when she told me about Torbett being jailed for his attacks against children in 1998. I recall mum having mentioned the name of one of the accusers at Torbett's trial at that time. I remembered and knew one of them well. He was the accuser who took my place as a Torbett victim. When Torbett told me when I sat in the back of his car that my time at the Boys' Club was over, it was that same young lad who sat in the front seat, the seat I had occupied for over a year, beside Torbett. The beast, it became evident had selected his next unfortunate victim even before he had thrown me out of the Boys' Club like a bag of rubbish. One thing became very clear though, thanks to mum, I knew now I was not alone. I wasn't the only one and perhaps, it hadn't been all my fault after all.

From then on, I took a little more notice, I had seen many other reports, not just Torbett, many other Boys' Club officials who had been involved with the Celtic's Boys' Club and had gone on to defile little dreamers. Each report made me angrier; it made me realise the whole subject was being covered-up by authorities and officialdom who all it appeared, had their own demons to hide. I realised it was unrealistic to expect my own individual case to have any effect in breaking down the barriers, after all, I would just have been repeating all those other poor children.

Of course, there is always the other damning reason for my silence. As each year passed without me coming forward and making a complaint, other young lives were being savaged. If I had committed to come forward earlier, I may well have been able to save some of those abused from their heinous fate. That guilt is not having helped sooner was as severe as any of the other guilts that had been forced into me.

I was silenced for 50 years. I am a single father, and at this time (2019) I had had my 10-year-old daughter, on my own, since she was 10 months old. She recently had a problem at school. She came home and we sat over our evening meal and discussed it. The issue was not of a serious enough nature that any discipline was necessary but rather an issue between her and a few friends. She had taken the side of, and supported a child who was being treated badly. The support she offered conflicted greatly with her own best friends' viewpoint. I asked why she had gone against her friends to help the child and she replied "Dad, I had to do the right thing".

It broke me knowing for 50 years that I had not. My daughter had her shower and went to bed to leave me alone hating myself for not having 'done the right thing' a long time beforehand. I felt I was as guilty as the perpetrators as my keeping my mouth shut had contributed to their success in remaining hidden.

I took my daughters thoughts on board and decided it was now the time for me "To do the right thing". If I didn't construct the courage now to do so then, I knew I never would. I was not in the best of health myself and my own mortality was under question, so the time had to be now.

Coincidentally, a few days later there was an article in Scotland's Daily Record writing about Celtic's continuing its claim of 'separate entity'. Of course, I felt I had information that would totally contradict that stance and I felt sick at the thought of probably 100's of child victims still being abused by this denial. Many victims simply wanted an apology and an acceptance that they were not, as they should have been, in a safe environment when with Celtic's Boys' Club, the opposite was indeed true. Celtic Boys'

Club for decades had been a playground for paedophiles.

Every child who signed for Celtic's Boys' Club were convinced they were a part of the Celtic family. Celtic's farcical denial was a horrendous response for the victims and their families, every denial forced further abuse onto the Celtic victims.

I had a strong urge to act on my daughter's advice and I picked up the telephone. I put a call through to the Solicitors mentioned in the article and asked for someone involved in the Celtic abuse scandal to call me back as I had some very important information for them. My disclosures appeared to be all new information for them. Aspects of my time at Celtic were previously unknown to the legal team and they welcomed my approach as my evidence if not dispelling the separate entity myth entirely, it went a long, long way to making it very doubtful. That was for a court to decide.

I felt an inner strength when I came off the phone. I hadn't felt that before. Of course, the telephone conversation was difficult and when I had to share the words "I was abused by Jim Torbett", I faltered, I couldn't get the words out and I became emotional, it took me a little while to compose myself and utter those words for the very first time. I had not expected that. For a long time thereafter, they were always difficult to speak when I opened to family, friends, the media, and the Police.

The Lawyers spoke about taking on my case and reporting the abuse to Police Scotland. I hadn't considered that at that time. I had no intention of going forward with, police statements, court actions, and all the unwanted drama that those would force onto me. My call was placed solely to give information and the thought of proceeding with anything else hadn't been given any thought.

At first it wasn't something that I wanted. As I thought deeper about it, without any coercion from anyone, it became clearer to me for my new information to be taken seriously and used in Courts of Law it would need me to be standing firmly behind it and to be prepared to give my testimony in Court. The advice I was given was that it was imperative I received some professional support, I needed to speak to those in a position to help me and for me to understand what I had went through and how to come to terms with it. After long and hard consideration, I asked the Lawyers to act on my behalf and I told them I would contact the Police to make a statement and a formal complaint.

I had no idea of course what I was letting myself in for. No idea that I would spend the next 4 years being called a liar, being accosted, and abused in the street by strangers who previously could well have been friends and abused on-line via social media from those who firmly believed in the 'big man's mantra' to keep the good name of Celtic clean at all times.

My lawyers arranged for my story to be discussed with a respected Journalist from the Daily Record. Keith McLeod visited my home and In October of 2019 that resulted in them printing a front-page story...

The Daily Record wrote... *Celtic Boys' club beast abused young player in toy shop while other man watched. Gordon Woods has bravely told how Jim Torbett attempted to rape him and then carried out a sex act.*

Gordon, who has the right to anonymity, has allowed us to use his name because he wants Torbett to know who he is. He said: "I want him to remember me, and I want him to think about what he did to me. I also want him to know that I will not be silenced anymore."

He says he was taken to the toy shop on Maryhill Road by Torbett on two occasions. And he claims that another man who was involved with Torbett – and Celtic Boys' Club – was present on one of the occasions in the 1960s.

Gordon said: "One of the times in the toy shop – when it was closed for lunch – Torbett took me into the storeroom or back room of the shop.

"He attempted to rape me and then carried out a sex act. I remember thinking that the door was open, and the other man was in the shop.

"I thought that was why the door was left open, so the other man could see in. I remember thinking, 'He's watching this' because there was no reason to leave the door open. Afterwards, Torbett carried on as if nothing happened."

Gordon says he believed he was with Celtic FC because the boys' club was viewed as one and the same. He recalled a trip to Dumfries for a match against a local team in 1968.

He said: "I overslept, and I knew I had missed the bus. I phoned the only available number I had as Torbett would have already left, Celtic Park, and spoke to one of the Celtic secretaries.

"I told them that I had missed the coach. Sometime later, the phone rang in the house, and it was the secretary I had spoken to.

"She asked if I could be at St Enoch Square underground station by 12 o'clock. A big burgundy car arrived and inside were Jock Stein and Sir Bob Kelly. Stein was driving.

"I went all the way to Dumfries with them. There was a big box next to me in the back. There was a brass latch and inside was two doors and it was the European Cup, or a replica of the European Cup. They were taking it to show the *boys of the team we were playing and the people down there. It was an honour to be in the same car as both these men."*

"I listen now to Celtic FC saying that Celtic Boys' Club was a totally separate organisation. Yet there was me having missed the bus, phoning Celtic Park, speaking to a Celtic FC secretary and then being picked up by the Celtic FC manager and chairman for a boys' club match in Dumfries."

"It enrages me the stance that Celtic are taking now. Whatever they are saying now, was definitely not the case at the time."

Gordon remembers attending Celtic Park for a match in September 1968 when Torbett summoned him to his car. Gordon says he would normally sit in the passenger seat, but on this occasion another boy was in that seat.

Gordon said he got in the back and Torbett said he thought their "friendship" should end.

He says he recognised the boy – who gave evidence against Torbett in the late 90s.

Gordon added: "This has affected me more in later years.

"I have now been able to explain this to my family, to let them know that this happened to me when I was very young and didn't really know what was happening to me. I'm glad I've

found the courage to speak. I hope that this will help others."

Boys' Club founder Torbett was jailed in November for six years, former general manager Frank Cairney, 84, was jailed in January for four years, fellow boys' club coach and Celtic FC man Jim McCafferty, 73, was jailed for six years and nine months, while former chairman Gerald King, 66, was convicted of preying on children at a Glasgow school but avoided jail.

In May, the Record revealed how Celtic FC cleared Torbett and Cairney of wrongdoing in 1986 – despite the club's claim of "separate entities" and that allegations first came to light in the early 1990s.

Gordon is a client of Thompsons Solicitors, which is seeking damages from Celtic FC for a string of clients.

Patrick McGuire from the firm said: "Mr Woods' harrowing account of abuse at the Celtic Boys' Club sheds new light on the scale of the abuse, as well as the close connections between the Boys' Club and Celtic.

"Particularly disturbing is his account of what happened to him at a toy shop frequented by his abuser.

"In telling his story publicly, Mr Woods has shown great courage which should be admired.

He, along with all the other survivors from Celtic and Celtic Boys' Club, want the club to take responsibility for the decades of abuse which happened on their watch and to show respect to those survivors by effecting quick and appropriate settlement of all legal actions."

20. POLICE, PROSECUTION AND SUPPORT

I contacted Police Scotland by phone and my details were taken and within a few days they visited me at home and a lady officer heard my complaint and took a few notes. As she had not been specially trained, she immediately advised me that a specialist officer would be needed to take any further details and that they would be in touch to take a full statement from me in due course. It wasn't in her remit to do so. I was in Police Scotland's system, again, but this time as the complainant. I knew I had done the right thing, but everything was moving too fast for me.

After a week or so I was contacted to arrange a visit to take my full statement and to progress with my complaint against Torbett. The date was arranged and a few days before the event, after experiencing a bout of sleep deprivation, due to recurring nightmares I pulled out citing problems at home and asked if everything could be put on hold for the moment. I had to clear my mind and ensure this is what I really wanted, in consideration of how it would affect my family and my friends going forward.

After a few months I made my decision. I called Police Scotland again and two specialist officers drove the 3 hours to my home from Glasgow and took my statement. The process took about 5 hours, and they were very patient and understanding.

A couple of weeks later they called and asked me if they could visit again to clarify certain points. They covered a lot of the same ground, the same questions, but they always got the same answers. I'm sure they were testing me to ensure my first statement was indeed accurate and true. It would have been easy of course to magnify, exaggerate, and invent scenarios when relating what had happened. I was very careful not to. It would only take one small detail to be discovered as untrue or not possible for the whole statement to come tumbling down. I told the truth about what happened, and when it happened as best as I could recall. Many of the incidents of abuse that I had experienced had to be kept to myself. Only the ones I could clearly remember were part of my police statement. Many things I had memories of but not complete. Snippets here and there that I could not swear under oath happened, as I could not recall them, and still can't, in their entirety. They left after a couple of hours with my statement which was now in the system and progressing, albeit very slowly.

The whole process was not as difficult as I had expected to be fair. It was difficult of course but the professionalism and calm approach taken by the specialist Police team certainly made things tolerable and within my reserved strength.

My statement had now been passed to another

specialist unit in the Springburn area of Glasgow responsible for handling all historic child abuse allegations. They got in touch and made an appointment once again to go over what I had told them. Another two hours of questions that they needed answers to for them to decide how to go forward.

I received a call from Police Scotland to advise that my files had been forwarded to The Procurator Fiscals office for a decision as to whether or not Torbett should be charged with his assaults on me. Two months later I got the call advising me Torbett has been visited in Dumfries prison, and formally charged with 4 counts of abusing me. Now the journey to justice had started in earnest and that thought terrified me.

What I didn't know at that time was although the Procurator Fiscals office had authorised the charges, I now had an uphill struggle convincing them to proceed to a court of law. Firstly, I had to convince the Fiscal (several stages) in the Sherriff Court and then again (several stages) convincing the Fiscals office in the High Court.

I had to endure umpteen phone calls from many individuals all trying to find fault with my story. That is in no way a criticism of the procedure, they had to be sure my story, how I told it, and my credibility would have to endure an assault from any defence counsel in the High Court.

A final telephone call, lasting well over an hour from the chief prosecutor at the High Court in Edinburgh concluded with him advising me that he was satisfied with my story, and he was proceeding to trial. Those few words meant so much to me and when I came off the phone, I cried with relief that those people, all in senior positions within the judicial system had believed me and my abhorrent experiences as a child.

It seems I was successful, the High Court beckoned.

Now I had to prepare myself for all that entailed. For the first time in over 50 years, I had to relate my abuse not just on a telephone to a faceless listener, to not just 1 individual journalist, not to perhaps 2 police officers or 2 people during any filming process. No, I had to tell a courtroom full of strangers, possibly 50+ individuals who were responsible to dissect and to question my every word, and to face the evil, devil of a man who abused my innocence.

Was I going to be able to garner the strength to see me through it all… You bet I was.

21. THE MAINSTREAM MEDIA

I was a very small voice when you consider who I was up against. A major world-famous sporting organisation with a following of perhaps millions throughout the world. Every one of those followers were expected to, and in the progress of time proved they intended to, ridicule, deny, and reject my story in its entirety. I expected social media abuse, I got it, but had never expected that abuse to reach the level it did. I was a liar, a fraud, a Rangers supporter just out to cause trouble, a Walter Mitty type character who had made the whole thing up and worse, to stay off the streets of Glasgow with my daughter. That continuous direct threat to me and my family's safety was concerning but only made me more determined. I would not be silenced. I needed help to raise my voice and the mainstream media would be required to make my story known to those who had, previously been unaware. Nothing I had said was fantasy, each claim was factual, and I was determined to prove it. In a court of law if needed.

The Lawyers had later put me in touch with Keith McLeod from The Daily Record and Alex Thompson from Channel 4. Both were very interested in certain aspects of my individual story that had not, until then, been revealed by anyone else. My information was virgin territory though it didn't take long for my Lawyers and Journalists to check out my statement and discover evidence to confirm its accuracy. Keith wanted to run the story and Alex Thomson wanted me to contribute to a forthcoming Channel 4 documentary on Child abuse in Scottish football. I was hesitant, of course, and gave it a lot of thought before I decided to give them the go ahead whilst retaining a part of my anonymity by giving them the authorisation to use my name only. At the time I hadn't spoken to family or friends, and I knew I would have to do so before anything became public.

I wrote to Keith at The Daily record advising him that I had decided that to have the strongest case going forward with any claim against Celtic Football Club for myself and the other victims or any complaint that may be made to the Police against Jim Torbett in the future, anonymity would not be conducive to the overall case success. I was now prepared to waive my right to anonymity and the Daily Record had my authority to use my name within the story proposed for publication.

I allowed my name to be used as I was determined that Torbett knew that it was me making the accusations against him. I wanted him and the many others who were in hiding to know that I had come forward. They would have been aware that I had new information and testimony that would lay to rest some of the myths that had surrounded the subject for decades. I wanted them to start squirming.

The first newspaper report used my name but no photographs showing my face as I had requested.

When the Channel 4 filming was due, I had already spoken to family members and friends, with their agreement I changed my mind, and waived my anonymity completely releasing my identity on both television and subsequent newspaper reports. I was confident this decision would add much more weight and belief to everything I had to say.

I was content with what I had done. A release was hoped for, but I was not prepared for the disgusting level of abuse that would subsequently be thrown in my direction.

One of my biggest disappointments since I came forward was when I was advised to listen to a BBC radio interview that John Beattie had with ex Celtic's Boys Club player Pat Nevin. Nevin, now a football media pundit and an ex-professional player had made, in my eyes, some inappropriate comments when the subject of child abuse at the boys' club was brought up during the interview.

I mentioned my annoyance on a telephone conversation with my lawyers the following day and they arranged for me to be interviewed for the John Beattie show on Radio Scotland to call-out Nevin on his comments. These interviews, as you would expect, are extremely difficult to do in consideration you are opening your heart and mind to a total stranger in a surreal environment. I took a few days to prepare myself and went ahead with the interview which was due to be aired a few days later. I was upset after the interview for a few days but eventually calmed and was pleased with my interview overall.

Days passed with no notification of the airing date. Days turned to weeks and then to months until I received a call from John Beattie to advise me his BBC bosses had ruled the interview was not to be broadcast. I was confused, felt terribly let down, and disgusted.

To say I was astonished is an understatement. How dare these people put a victim through what they did and then refuse to air? The BBC in Scotland seem to have learned nothing from the Jimmy Saville scandal when a paedophile was operating within the BBC for decades and covered up by the hierarchy there. Here, they were doing the same with my own situation and covering-up all that I had to say. Disgraceful but not unexpected or surprising with the BBC being who they are and who they deem it important to protect.

I have done other radio interviews with Adrian Goldberg in the UK, with Gary Johnson for Australian radio, Ed Opperman for American listeners. On all occasions I was treated with the understanding and respect the subject matter more than deserves. Not one other person or organisation did I speak to treated me with the irrelevance that the BBC was to exhibit.

The press overall has been absent from my case and found it appropriate, for their reasons, only known to them, to ignore my plea for help to publicise my trauma and help to secure safety for children in the future. Many ran a short story, all taking the details from The Daily Record story. To this date, only a few other journalists from any of the Scottish newspapers have been in touch to ask if they can help, the Scottish Daily Express and The Scottish Sun have started to take an interest.

They all have their reasons, though I suspect they all have the same reason. To protect the 'good name' of a certain football club. The very same 'protect the good name' that had been instrumental for decades in facilitating the abuse of many, many, innocent young lives.

I make no apology for using mainstream media, podcast interviews, broadcasted interviews, and social media, amongst others, throughout the UK and across the globe, to condemn that club and to embarrass it for its response to the claimant's allegations. In my opinion Celtic Football Club has shown itself to be as abhorrent, as evil, as complicit, in the decades of abuse as those perpetrators were. Some perpetrators have had to answer to it, Celtic Football Club must do so too!

22. MY CHILDREN

My own, first two children, grew up totally unaware of what their father had gone through. They were both in their mid-forties when I came forward and it was necessary to sit them down and explain everything to them.

My son, who I hadn't seen for some time although he lives nearby, felt a need to distance himself from it all. He was reticent to watch, listen to, or read the reports as I assume he felt the content would be upsetting. I, of course, respect his decision on that and can fully understand his stance. I'm not sure how I would have reacted had my own father opened up to me with a similar scenario.

My oldest daughter's first comment was 'It explains a lot dad'. I didn't ask her to expand on that as I am sure the explanation that was not sought would most certainly have been on negative matters that she would have experienced in her life. Negative experiences that I had been party to and ones that I could never have forgiven myself if I had known how much they had hurt my beautiful daughter as she matured. I didn't want to intrude into her memories by asking her to furnish me with an expansion nor did I need any more guilt thrust in my direction at this stage.

My youngest daughter, who at the time was 10

years old when I came forward was only told that a bad man did bad things to me when I was a wee boy and had touched me where he wasn't allowed to.

She didn't ask for more details but did ask one day if she could read my twitter timeline where I had been highlighting my issues. Of course, I refused telling her it wasn't something a young child should be reading. Despite her pleas, I stood my ground and wouldn't allow her to do so. Within a day or two, she had joined twitter on her own, with a fake profile, and had started following me, giving her access to the whole sordid story. I discovered her actions early, blocked her, and warned her any repetition would result in her iPad being confiscated for a month. As far as I know, she has kept her promise not to do it again!

As my children grew up, I found it increasingly more difficult to offer them the attention and love every little heart need from their dad. My difficulty was being able to express my love for them. Of course, they meant everything to me, and I worked hard, each and every day, to hopefully give them the life that I had been denied in my early years. I wanted them to be happy, to have the material things that had escaped me, the things that are only important if you don't have them. More important than anything else I wanted them to be safe, unhurt, emotionally secure and to be loved by their parents in a way that it would be obvious to them and leave them in no doubt that they were adored and respected.

As they searched and asked their dad for the attention, they craved I experienced a growing inability to respond. Playing games, trips out and the obligatory walks were fine but any activity that demanded a closeness, contact, or consoling them was difficult and became increasingly so as they got older each day. I was very aware of my feelings and knew where they were emanating from but couldn't find a way to fight it and dispel the memories causing the issues.

I was still adamant that my secrets should remain just that and I certainly was not open to discussing my fears with anyone. Not even my wife who I had met when I was 18 years old, married at 19-years-old and who had always given me everything I could have wanted from a partner. She had not put a foot wrong, a loving wife, and a loving mother who unknowingly had had to take a portion of my responsibilities without even realising it or being aware a problem even existed.

After the birth of our two children together part of my job in those days as a salesman was to be away from home overnight, sometimes for up to a week at a time. I had to cover a territory from Tayside to the far north of Scotland including the island of Orkney. Those breaks from family life did me the world of good. Often trips away would coincide with me feeling my very worst and unable to cope with the many issues I faced and from the attentions my two little ones sought.

I was successful and every month of every year for the whole of the seven years I was with this company seen me as the top UK salesman out of a sales force of approximately 100+ personnel. Unfortunately, at the conclusion of my seven years, I made one of the most life-changing decisions I have made. I felt my challenges had been met and needed a new direction and sought employment elsewhere. Within a month I had secured a position with a household name, an international company with a massive increase in salary, a far better company car, and a stimulating position to test my abilities.

However, my new position had one major drawback and that was the need to work away was removed from my routine and the area covered easily worked from home. This, in the coming years, would prove disastrous for the family unit as I desperately tried to overcome the constant niggle that enveloped me, and which grew to a level that I was unable to confront successfully. My occasional escape was no longer available to me, and decisions had to be made.

I was painfully missing the normality and the escape that my previous employment offered. As the months passed, I became more conscious of the difficulties I was experiencing in being the father I wanted to be. As my children neared the age, I knew in my heart would make me most uncomfortable, I made the decision to leave the matrimonial home and subsequently my wife, she and I divorced. Whether my marriage would have survived without the memories that controlled me I will, of course, never know.

To this day my wife and I live close to each other, see each other occasionally and I would like to think we have a good relationship considering all that happened.

I would expect all that has recently been exposed will answer some of her questions, I hope so as it is important, she realises that all the blame lay on me.

I have, at this point in time, still not sat down with my children and offered them the explanations that I know they deserve. It is painful to me and perhaps they will allow me the opportunity one day to be my sorriest and ask for their forgiveness. Hopefully, they will understand.

Maybe they will take the time to read my words?

23. PRESS STATEMENTS.

I was asked to write several statements to the press prior to them publishing a story and mention some of them here as it is a measure of how the press handled a very difficult story.

Daily Record Statement Submitted – October 2019

Only since I came forward in late 2109 as a victim of Child Sexual Abuse, I am pained at the fact that for the first time in my 65+ years, and with a heavy heart, I am ashamed of my country of birth. Not all its people but its complicit authorities over many decades, and the club I supported and played for as a child! It really hurts!

The effect of the abuse I suffered whilst at Celtic's Boys' Club has been overwhelming since I decided to come forward in September 2019. I felt a need to right the wrongs that have gone undisclosed for over 4 decades. I came forward after 50 years with a positive view knowing I was strong enough to make known, waiving my anonymity, of my abhorrent experiences. That strength, to my cost, was unfortunately overestimated. I am more than determined than ever, regardless, to see the fight for justice continue until those to blame are uncovered and apologies issued to everyone affected.

The dream I was promised in 1967 had nothing

to do with my footballing ability, my initial trial ended in failure with only an intervention by my abuser allowing me a reprieve. I never played a 'competitive' game for Celtic's Boys' Club. The Celtic dream which was promised had sinister connotations from the very start and has morphed from a dream into a nightmare of massive proportions. I was a target from my very first experience with Celtic's Boys' Club.

I am photographed holding a trophy that I had no involvement in winning, but my abuser wanted me in the photograph. I am seen standing, a frequent event, with the Celtic Manager, the Celtic Chairman, Jim Torbett, and the Celtic European Cup-winning Captain. I now know my abuser wanted the photograph as his own 'Trophy'.

This surely ridicules the Celtics stance of a separate entity. Their statement is outrageous and calculated prevarication. Nothing could be further from the truth. Every boy who signed for Celtic's Boys' Club knew they were getting involved directly with Celtic Football Club. We were joining the Celtic Family. We had the respect of our own families, parents, siblings, and extensions to those who were so proud and excited that one of their own had an opportunity with Celtic F.C.

I trained at Barrowfield; I was involved in a Celtic Boys' Club games at Parkhead (once in front of a full house of 69,000 in September 1968) and received complimentary stand tickets for Celtic Football Club matches regularly. I was often in the company of many Celtic Football Club officials and players, these facts only endorsed our beliefs that we were Celtic Football Club we at the boys' club were often utilised to even sell the match day programmes at Celtic Park at home games. To be eventually thrown out of the Club, discarded not for footballing reasons but for standing up for myself, for asking for the abuse to end, was a further degradation and one that haunted me for many decades. My dream had been smashed to smithereens in a flash, perhaps if I had allowed the abuse to continue my dream would have come true? Those thoughts occupied my mind for many years on what might have been. I was 14 years old, and my life then took a totally different course than I had previously planned. Since I was 8 or 9 years old, I wanted to be a Vet or an Author, or to join the R.A.F. but my heinous football experience changed all that. My life would have been lived very differently without my Celtic involvement.

Celtic Football Club's persistent denial has left the victims feeling abused again and again and again, not just physically, but increasingly mentally and emotionally. Every denial is a kick in the teeth and further abuse of the 100's of boys who know the clock cannot be turned back but they can still, even at this late stage, be given the justice they so rightly need and deserve. The victims need the abuse to end once and for all. The abuse started in the 1960s and yet here we are in the 2020s (6 decades later) with those same victims still being abused on a regular basis with every denial from Celtic Football Club every time they open a newspaper, watch a sport programme, or see a Celtic Strip being worn in the street whilst they go about their daily lives as best they can... they are reminded.

Unfortunately, Celtic is a massive name, so the victims are not allowed to forget even though many others deem it acceptable to do so. That includes the Scottish Government who have done all they can to block a full public inquiry into what happened at Celtic for 4 decades. They appear to be trading votes to turn a blind eye on the abuse of innocent children on their countries soil. Scotland is not a good country to be born in if you expect justice for child abuse victims!

Daily Record Statement Submitted – March 2020

After coming forward initially in October of 2019 it became clear that to me that many people just did not understand, perhaps they didn't want to, the impact child sexual abuse had on its victims in the long term. The victims, sadly, live with their experience for the rest of their lives and this same horrendous experience   most   certainly horrifically affects everyone around them, parents, friends, siblings, their own children, and future relationships.

I felt it was important for the blind-folded public to realise and acknowledge how a young child can be forced into a life of confusion and how they can never, even as adults, return to normality. The head in the sand authorities need to read the book and then explain their despicable inaction and ignorance of the facts for decades.

Due to time and space constraints on media my story wasn't being heard as it should be. A book of my total experience from child to pensioner was the way forward to educate those who needed educated. My book will relay who I was as a child, my dreams and aspirations before the abuse, and the innocence I had at that time. It explains my time at Celtic's Boys Club, and it will clarify some issues that until now have been mired with inaccuracies and confusion. The book will further explain how my abuse threw me into a life of compunction, self-abuse, alcohol, crime, and an inability to love my children as I should have been allowed to do. It involves the sadness when my parents passed with the guilt of what had happened to me.

I came forward after a chance chat with my 10-year-old daughter with regards a problem she had at school. She gave me her reason for the problem arising, "Dad, I had to do the right thing". It broke me knowing for 50 years that I had not. I thought about it long and hard and after explaining to my family and friends, with great difficulty, for the first time in over 50 years what had happened to me I also did the right thing and came forward.

If the book helps just one victim, gives one victim the strength to come forward, allows just one victim to realise they are not at fault and not alone, it has been worth it!

Daily Record Statement Submitted – July 2023

When I first came forward, I had a difficult time recounting to others when and what had happened during my time at Celtic Boys' Club, clearly and detailed. With time and space constraints within media it was obvious my story and its background were not being told or explained fully but rather in at times confusing snippets.

One piece of advice I received from several people was to write everything down when I was going through difficult patches as it would be beneficial to my mental health and ability to accept my abhorrent experiences. When I did so it became apparent that writing the book may be the way forward to tell my story completely with

197

a full explanation as to how certain controversial issues came to being.

I decided to start writing the book in 2020 and had it mostly completed by the end of that year. For legal reasons it has been held back until after the criminal trial that took place in April of 2023. With the occasional update as issues reared their head.

I'm aware the book will have a very limited audience due to its content and subject matter, but this has never been about selling books, it has been about putting a victim's whole story out there for people to understand, to educate, and to hopefully give others the strength to come forward. I felt it important to tell the story in its entirety even if only to a small section of the public. Only. Perhaps to those readers interested in a) The Celtic Boys' Club Scandal, b) To those affected by child sexual abuse, and very importantly, c) As a vehicle to persuade others, due to my own success, to seriously consider speaking out and seeking their own route to justice.

We must break this cycle of silence.

The book explains the help, understanding and respect shown to me throughout my fight for justice and is a solid indicator to those on the brink of coming forward to do so, and to remove the dark sinister cloak that has enveloped their lives for many years.

If I can do it, so can they, there is always a way forward regardless of how dark the road may look at the start. The book includes advice from Project 90/10, written by Emma-Jane Taylor to encourage those who need to get in touch to do so.

If, by writing the book I can help one single victim who has become a survivor, to come forward and release their misplaced guilt, shame, and embarrassment then it will have been a success.

24. PROJECT 90/10

As well as telling my own story and to try to also clarify certain points with regards the association between Celtic Football Club and Celtic Boys' Club during my time there, it was also my intention to address the issue of surviving victims who had not yet made the decision to come forward, despite possibly feeling the need to do that. I would hope my journey and success in securing justice over my abuser will encourage others to come forward.

#notmyshame Project 90-10 is a charitable organisation headed by Emma-Jane Taylor and I have asked her to add to my words via a contribution to explain to you how they may be able to help anyone intending to speak out.

On average, *90% of children being sexually abused know their perpetrator, a stat that many still don't want to understand more of, and a stat that fuels my advocacy and campaigning.*

Every-day survivors of child sexual abuse write to me, sharing their difficult story and asking for advice and support, I feel honoured to hear every story. Many survivors feel trapped by the silence surrounding the conversation of child sexual abuse, some are tired of it, but all are generally feeling unheard because of this complex subject.

Over the last 6 years I have found myself in a position of speaking out about my own personal story, often finding myself wanting to do more to help other survivors; I always said if my story could give one person hope, then it will have all been worth it, it is why I wrote my debut book, **Don't Hold Back**, and why I campaign, take part in awareness campaigns, speak professionally and more recently launched Project 90/10.

Project 90/10 is a charity set up in March 2023 for the public benefit. The charities focus is to educate, raise awareness and protect children from child sexual abuse. We are creating educational packs for schools, safe-guarding teams, clubs, and various children-activities to encourage young people to understand the importance of healthy relationships, how to trust - *or understand what trust means* - and how to recognise when to question, speak out and know who to speak to. We are excited about the work we are doing, and the impact we are already having in the safe-guarding space, as well as the awareness we are raising across the UK.

Project 90/10 charity is a vehicle for influential attitude and action change through education and awareness campaigns in the area of child sexual abuse. Our mission is not only to offer clear protection, support, and solution to children and parents who have already suffered, but key education and innovative awareness to current demographics and other important sectors of society ensuring prevention rather than cure. In an ever quickly changing world Project 90/10 are wholly committed and passionate to change the way this pivotal issue is averted, healed, treated, and supported.

In May 2023 I launched the **#NotMyShame** campaign, my slogan and new range of merchandise that I hope will turn the tables on the shame of Child Sexual Abuse! My hope is that this message will give survivors their voices, empower them to feel heard, and to remind them that the shame of child sexual abuse isn't theirs, and never has been, they were just children - it was NOT their fault. The blame lands solely at the door of those that have hurt children in this way.

One day it just hit me, *why shouldn't I wear a tee-shirt that exposes someone else's secret?* Like millions of others, I've harboured someone else's secret for most of my life. I do understand why I did so, but now I don't want to. Quite simple really. **It is Not My Shame**. I am proud to share the #notmyshame slogan, empowering survivors and turning the tables on a very difficult conversation, that for the best part of my life has been kept in the dark.

In my opinion, we see many great causes emblazoned across merchandise across the world, but nothing on child sexual abuse. It's like every other cause means something and the conversation of child sexual abuse doesn't.

Wearing a tee-shirt that shares the silence of child sexual abuse, is not comfortable. But I know wearing it has given me confidence, along with many others, it has encouraged more conversations, allowed more awareness around the work I do, my campaigning and the importance of lifting the lid on the stigma of this conversation. I want survivors and supporters to wear their merchandise with confidence, and without shame.

Since launching in May, the campaign has already been seen in America, Canada, Australia, Dubai, Europe, Pakistan, South Africa, and the UK, with many soap stars/ pop stars/ journalists all standing up to support this movement.

The #notmyshame merchandise gives a charitable donation to Project 90/10.

On the 1st of May 2024 #notmyshame is

marking a joint 1st anniversary celebration with Project 90/10 to raise the roof on the conversation of child sexual abuse around the world – everyone is welcome. For more information you can follow the campaign on twitter @notmyshameuk to keep up to date with news and events or subscribe to my newsletters via my website www.emmajanetaylor.com

Just remember, you are not (and never have been) alone....

Emma-Jane Taylor

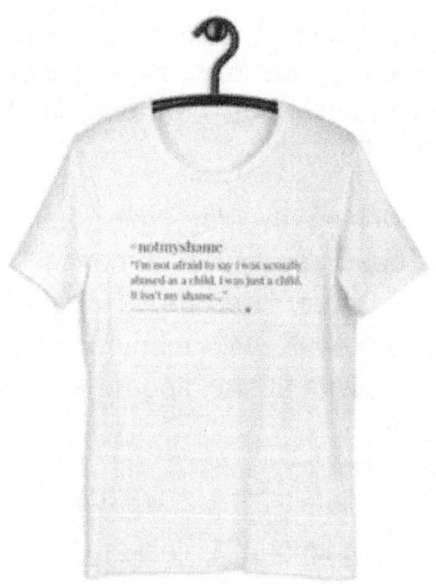

#notmyshame

25. CRIMINAL JUSTICE

Criminal justice for victims seems a long way away, and it is. That lengthy road however should never deter an individual from seeking justice. To put their abuser behind bars, to take back the control and the power those bastards take from children and continue to do so long into adulthood is well worth the determined effort. You don't have to be a hero, you don't have to be brave, you only have to be determined and truthful.

Many think that they will not be believed, and they give up before they even start. I thought that too, for 50 years!

But let me tell those wavering on the brink whether or not to speak out... you will be believed. The experts estimate that a very small percentage of abuse claims are false. Those that are false are generally discovered very quickly. The greatest asset you have to be believed is that you know the truth. You know what happened and the one speaking the truth will always speak the same truth no matter how often any particular question is presented to them.

As I said, I doubted I would be believed for so long that any other outcome seemed impossible. That hatred for what happened, that dark cloud over me, that sense of my necessary acceptance, and my need for silence, the continued silence surrounding child sexual abuse everywhere was an indication to me that it was probably better to keep my mouth shut.

That was until one day I was pushed over the edge.

I told myself to speak out, shout out, speak to anyone and everyone who would listen, and do not be afraid to do so. All those previous fears were overtaken by what is right, overtaken by a sense of what I had to do to right those wrongs, not just for me but also for many silent individuals who had not yet been pushed over the edge. Maybe, if I could just show them that there is a way out, there is a route to peace, there is a route to removing the guilt, the shame, and the embarrassment then it's important for me to do so.

My own reaction to being pushed over the edge saw a determination, an awakening within me that now was the time to speak out. Now it was time to seek address, an apology for my life and the lives of so many others close to me, my family members, my friends having been ruined. Again, I was one of the lucky ones, my edge saw me start a very long, very arduous fight for justice, others weren't so lucky. Their edge saw them end their lives and that organisation has blood on their hands. Many young victims saw that as their only way out to stop their haunting memories of Celtic's Boys' Club.

My road began in September of 2019 when I read that article in the media about Celtics denial and in my eyes, their continual abhorrent abuse of their victims (claiming this 'separate entity' nonsense) and I had spoken to my daughter and listened to her wisdom.

I telephoned the solicitors mentioned in the article to let them know I had hopefully some very important evidence for them. That was the first time I had spoken to anyone since 1968 about the abuse, and even then, that had been with my abuser! I realised very early in the call that I had great difficulty uttering those words, "I was abused by Jim Torbett", so I didn't. I think the words I used were 'I suffered at the Celtic Boys' Club too". It was many months later that I could actually say those words without breaking down, once was in front of my 45-year-old daughter when I was required to confide in her and to tell her I was speaking out. It was the first time in her life she had saw her father cry.

That fear of not being believed had also started its journey. As I spoke to my first contact at the lawyers there was no comment nor questioning that would indicate I was not being believed. That was to continue throughout my revelations. *I was believed*. I later spoke to Police Scotland, I spoke to them for a total of 9 hours, *I was believed*. I spoke to the media, to experienced, well respected journalists, *I was believed*. I spoke to many levels of Procurator Fiscals office representatives in firstly, the Sherriff Court arena and then the High Court arena, each of those individuals had no negative response to what I had to say, *I was believed*. The final telephone call was from a very senior representative from the High Court Procurators Fiscals Office. This was my last hurdle and I talked with him for over an hour. At the end of that conversation, I heard the words... *"Mr Woods, we will be going forward with the trial of James Torbett". I was believed.*

Now I had to put my trust in the truth and 15 members of a jury in the High Court on a date and place to be determined. *I prayed I would be believed*.

After what seemed to be an eternity, I received the date for Torbett's trial. It was still 9 months away but as I had already waited 50 years to confront him that was not an issue. A floating trial at the Inverness High Court on 18th April 2023 was the date set. The trial was held in Inverness, not as many people thought as a convenience to the complainants, but due to the fact the defence thought a fair trial may not be possible if held in Glasgow or Edinburgh, so Inverness was chosen, and once again, I had no problem with that. It was imperative that Torbett was given a fair trial, with a jury unaware of his past and who would arrive at their decision on the evidence presented to them in the 7 days that the trial imposed on their lives. There could be no doubt attached that the bastard got a fair trial and that whatever the jury decided at the end of their deliberations would be a fair and correct one based only on the evidence they heard.

I was told the trial was to start on Tuesday 18th April 2023. It was normal for that first day to be taken up by the selection and the 'swearing in' of the jury and other legal preparations. I was asked to travel on the 18th and be prepared to take the stand first on the 19th at 10am.

I arranged for my daughter to be looked after by friends for a week although I didn't expect to be away that long. I had no idea what my state of mind would be on my return so felt it safer for her to be away a bit longer than necessary, preferably until after the jury had made their long-awaited decision. That way she would not be subjected to a worried, irritable, angry, grumpy old bastard! The dog was homed by my older daughter, so everything was in order, and it was time to face my abuser in a Court of Law. The nearly four-year emotional fight had culminated in and was dependent on the next few days and the 15 strangers who were being forced to listen to my evidence.

The journey to Inverness was about 100 miles and expected to take a couple of hours. Due to my frame of mind and the probability of concentration lapses I decided to take my time and enjoy the drive. I don't think my speed was ever over 50mph so was able to switch the car from 'Sports Mode' to 'Eco Mode'.

I arrived in Inverness mid-afternoon and as I had received threats on social media saying my car would be attacked, I went straight to the Court only to discover there was no secure parking available for anyone other than the Court staff. I had just passed an Arnold Clark car sales showroom on the roundabout immediately prior to the Court and did a 'U' turn back to their forecourt. I went into the offices and explained the situation to them that I needed a safe place to put the car for a few hours. I explained I had bought the car from them the previous year in Aberdeen and that my annual service was due with them in a months time. They instantly agreed and asked me for the keys. They told me they would put the car into their secure guarded compound themselves and when I returned, they would bring it out back to me. Thank you, Arnold Clark, Inverness. Fortunately, the hotel I booked into later that day had secure parking, so Mr Clark's services was not required for the rest of my stay as taxis took me to and from the courtroom.

The taxi arrived at the hotel at 9.20am to take me to the court and I was immediately directed to the rear of the building where the witnesses and jurors would enter, removed from the eyes of the public and those who may well be the accused in the main foyer.

Torbett was to face 4 charges (could easily have been 44 had my fragile memory had more clarity), 2 charges of indecent assault and 2 charges of using lewd, indecent, and libidinous practices towards me, as well as touching me on the body while I was asleep at a flat in Sighthill.

Victim support were there to meet me and from the moment I entered the building until the moment I left in late afternoon they were by my side. They were supportive in every way, they explained the process, kept me informed on what I could expect to happen and always ensured I was comfortable and as far as they could, kept me stress free, positive, and determined.

During my wait I was introduced to my counsel, Advocate depute Angela Gray KC, who kept me right as to what to expect in the courtroom itself, the positioning of the opposing legal teams, the witness box, the dock, the jury, the usher, and the judge. She explained that a screen would be in place to shield me from the defendant's view. I would be unable to see him, but he could still see me (as is his right) via a camera linking to a screen in front of him. The screen is to avoid any distress or discomfort to the witness that having sight of the accused might bring.

She asked if I had any questions, I had! I asked her if the screen could be removed? She advised me that the screen was important and that she recommended I keep it in place. I told her that the defendant had had control of and power over my life for 50 years. I wanted that to end this very day, I wanted to show him that he had no power over me now. The power that had silenced me for nearly my whole life was being taken back and I wanted him to have to look into my eyes and I into his when I gave my evidence and when I spoke my whole truth. It was removed with an instruction to signal the victim support if I wanted to have it re-instated.

I then became aware that the actual trial had started on the Monday (17th) and that the jury had been selected and sworn in a day earlier due to a previous trial having finished early. It had been deemed unnecessary to inform me and have me change my plans to come up to Inverness a day early and the Tuesday had been used to take the testimony of several witnesses via video-link.

I took the stand mid-morning of the 18th and victim support sat immediately to my right just outside the witness box and had made me aware to signal to her if there were any problems. The usher sat immediately to my left, again just outside the witness box, he had already asked me if I wanted to take the oath or affirmation. I took the oath.

So, for the first time in my experience of speaking out I was now in the scenario that I had to open up to a room full of strangers in the most formal of possible arenas. I took my seat before I had a sip of water and readied myself.

I broke down on the stand just the once. When I spoke about my parents, when and how I found out they had known about the abuse. It upset me because no amount of justice will ever remove my haunting thought that my mother had that animal on her mind a few hours before she passed away and how my father was taken within days afterwards without me having the opportunity to talk with him, after deciding it was imperative I did so.

My first few hours on the stand were filled with my own KC asking me to explain to the jury the events that had taken place that brought me to that place, that day. I did so but in my mind, I had excluded everyone else in the room. I spoke directly to and rarely took my eyes off my questioner, again, I was relating my story on a one-to-one basis and not to a room full of strangers. I only looked away to turn to my right to ensure Torbett was paying attention, I was aware of his penetrating stare as I spoke. Each time I did so he either turned away or looked down. The bastard refused to meet me eye to eye. I saw a coward, an abuser of children, I saw a broken, powerless, excuse of a man, a child-rapist, a paedophile and evil in his every ounce of being. Yes, I saw evil, and it made me feel good, I felt strong, I knew I should be proud of myself. It made me nauseous that I was actually breathing the same air as this bastard.

My cross-examination began by counsel asking me what I did for a living. I told him I had retired but still continued to run my small graphic design business from a home office.

He paraphrased and confirmed my answer then asked if I was or was not an author. I said I was not. He asked if I was or was not a writer. I said I was not. The reasoning behind this questioning was to become very clear as the trial progressed, evil works in mysterious ways!

The defence KC looked at me once or twice between questions and smiled and as anyone would do, I smiled back. Then I thought something was amiss. Why did he think it appropriate to smile? I realised that as he had his back to the jury, they would not have seen him smile at me and it may well have looked to them that I was being flippant or disrespectful smiling at the defence KC between questions. His smiles henceforth were met with a serious look and his game was sussed… Of course, that is if there had been a game at all as perhaps, he really was just being nice? I'll never know for sure; paranoia can be so dangerous.

He continued a line of questioning which did not cover, in any way, shape or form the actual abuse that I, at that time, had alleged had taken place. He had no questions on my time at Celtic Boys' Club. He did ask about the toy shop but with general questions without mention of the abuse allegations that happened there.

I sat slightly confused as I had expected a far greater level of cross-examination and it had yet to show itself. I don't know if the judge was getting annoyed or not, but he asked counsel if he had many more questions to ask as time was moving on and there was only 45 minutes until the court closed for the day. Council for the defence answered that he had considerably. more questions and that it would certainly take longer than the time left on the clock that day. The judge then made the decision to adjourn, and I was asked to return to the stand at 10am the following morning.

The taxi arrived and took me to the courtroom. I had booked out of the hotel the previous day assuming my time in Inverness would not be extended so I had had to check-in again to lay my head for another night. I was prepared.

At 10am the usher took me up from the secure victim support offices to the witness waiting area and I took a seat, every time I sat down, my legs went numb, I had to stand and walk about to keep the blood flowing.

After a few minutes I was told there would be a delay of about 15 minutes due to legal argument. Then another 30 minutes delay, for the same on-going reason, so we made the decision to retreat and go back to Victim Support. At 11.45 I was, eventually recalled and took my seat in the witness box once again after a delay of 1 hour and 45 minutes. I hadn't been made aware of the substance of the legal argument that had taken so long.

The cross-examination continued although it seemed to me without teeth. At times I felt he was mocking my evidence; I kept my cool as my evidence was strong and Torbett's defence was not. It was very clear by this point that the defence was avoiding cross-examining me on the alleged sexual offences and even my time at Celtic Boys' Club, he didn't want to re-visit my evidence for some reason.

I was called a liar and he suggested evidence I had given was not the same as I had given to the police in my original statement. He made, and continued to make, a very strong issue on this. I asked if it was permissible for me to view that section of my statement and permission was given. The Usher gave me the document and directed me to the page in question. Unbelievably I was able to show the court, and more importantly the jury, that my evidence in court was exactly what I had told the police. I believe the issue had been manufactured although maybe I'm wrong, and he was just mistaken.

When I said initially, I had only called the lawyers to give them information and that I had no intention at that time of coming forward he asked if I had been encouraged to come forward. I said no, I had been advised. The same question was asked about the call to police, the conversation with journalists, my speaking to my family, each and every time I corrected him when he alluded to me having been encouraged, in that I confirmed over and over again that I had been advised and that I had never been encouraged.

Three questions were asked that with a yes or no answer that left me open to looking unreliable. I asked three times to expand on my answer to clarify the question, three times I was refused being told 'we will come back to that', he never did go back to the question but I'm sure the jury noticed.

The defence KC asked me if I was really asking the jury to believe that the complicated procedure of manufacturing the encapsulated medals was done in the defendant's own home and not in the toy shop where there were presumably better conditions and would have been more spacious? "There were no facilities in the toy shop for children to be taken into his bed" was my reply.

The one other major part of the defence cross-examination that I was not happy about was when he questioned me on my website which mentions my proposed book in detail. Still images of the website were shown to the jury, the images only showed small parts of the website that spoke about the book. Other areas of the website were deliberately covered up by defence counsel so the jury could not see them. The covered parts were all about my campaign for a judicial review, questioning the SFA report in its entirety, my campaign for mandatory reporting, my campaign for Westminster Government to intervene if and when cross-border trafficking of children was confirmed, nor the many links to TV, radio, documentaries, press reports, and interviews. All these were conveniently hidden to show my website to be nothing like it actually was and its true purpose concealed from the jury. He paused, and showed the jury a snippet on the site, and asked if I had written, on the website, that extract from the book which called Torbett a filthy bastard. "Yes", I replied proudly.

Another grey area of defence counsels' credibility came when again, my occupation was brought up. I was asked why I had said I was not a writer or an author when asked. Had I been untruthful with my reply? Had I lied? My reply was that nothing I had written to date had been published and as such I had no right to call myself either. He disagreed and suggested again I had misled the court and that I was a liar.

To me that question was loaded and no matter how I had answered it would have had consequences. If I had said yes, I'm a writer or yes, I'm an author his response would have been the same. That I had lied, and that I was neither a writer nor an author because no work had ever been published so why had I lied to the court. Heads he wins, tails I lose. I must admit I froze momentarily at this point, and as that particular question passed, I was angry with myself for asking permission to expand, I should have done so anyway and waited to be stopped or reprimanded 'just answer the question', as I should also have done with the other loaded questions. But I didn't expand, obviously the jury agreed with me anyway and probably saw my frustration.

One final point, and how he knew I have no idea. Defence counsel tried to insinuate that I had been in contact with a previous Torbett victim via my direct messages on Facebook. That victim had given evidence on my behalf at the current trial. I was able to reassure him that the contact he spoke about was not the person he thought it was but was his son. I hoped he would push it further as I would have been able to introduce to the court my phone showing the exact conversation where I told him on first contact that I could not discuss the case or evidence in any way but can only talk about things in general. Talking about any aspect of the criminal trial was way out of bounds. Defence counsel let it go and immediately rested his case with no more questions.

To say the least I was astonished. No questions about the alleged assaults and sexual abuse, no questions about my time at Celtic Boys' Club, no questions on anything I would have deemed relevant other than trying to, without success, blacken my name and make me out to have been lying.

When the trial ended on the Friday at 4pm the jury were retired for the weekend. On the Monday they would hear final arguments and be directed by the judge before being allowed to commence their deliberations. My 4-year fight was now out of everybody's hands except those 15 people who I had no option other than to put my faith in.

On the Friday evening I received a phone call from a concerned individual and as the trial had ended the caller was able to tell me why there had been legal argument on the Thursday morning. Defence counsel had attempted to collapse the case due to my being an unreliable witness and having lied to the court on the

Wednesday afternoon. It seems defence counsel had argued that as I had already started to write my book, I should have described myself as a writer and/or an author and not a graphic designer during some of the earlier questioning. I've covered that in a previous paragraph but defence counsel's attempt to collapse the case with that reasoning had obviously been dismissed by the judge and the trial was, quite rightly, allowed to continue.

So, the defence had put up no defence. They had nothing to counter my allegations other than accusations and an inept attempt to discredit me which had failed in every way.

They had no defence because I spoke the truth. They had no defence because everything I accused Torbett of doing, he had done. They had no defence because their abhorrent strategy of discrediting me had failed, it failed because it had no substance.

However, due to hearing about the attempt to collapse the trial I began to doubt myself. I thought I had let myself down. I had spent 4 years preparing for this and had not been strong enough to complete the fight. I had made a terrible mistake at the worst possible time, and Torbett could well take advantage of that few seconds when I should have clarified my career status. I was distraught all weekend. I sat alone for 3 days, I never left the house, no calls were taken, and I doubt I actually ate anything, I honestly can't recall, and I spoke to no-one except myself, and I really did not give myself an easy time of it. For the first time in many a year I must admit I sobbed and had steadied myself for a negative decision the following week, thankfully I had made the decision for my daughter to stay away until after the verdict, and that had proven to be a wise decision.

I had pre-arranged as requested for a photographer from the Daily Record to visit on the Tuesday morning to take a few snaps as they intended running a story immediately the verdict was announced. He had arrived on time, and we were having a chat when my phone rang. I asked if the photographer minded if I took the call as I recognised the number to be a journalist from The Scottish Sun reporter, Stuart Patterson… Unanimous, Guilty, On All Four Counts he told me!

I handed the telephone to the photographer, put my head in my hands and broke down.

I have, as I write, a little time yet to wait to fully savour Torbett's conviction. He was due for early release in May of 2024 but will now serve an additional three years. Only in May of 2024 will he start to serve the 3 years in prison imposed for abusing me and on that day, I will raise a glass and thank all who made his conviction possible… The Scottish Government, Police

Scotland, Procurator Fiscals office, the Judiciary, Victim Support and especially that brave man who testified for the prosecution at Torbett's trial, I will forever be in his debt.

James Torbett will be 80 years old when he is eventually released onto the streets, he is still, in my opinion, a danger to children and must be watched carefully. Perhaps he will breathe his last breath in prison? That wouldn't be a bad thing. All this, of course, unless other Torbett victims, and there are many, decide to come forward and take back their own power. If those silent victims 'do the right thing' for themselves, and for others, see him charged and convicted for his evil crimes against them, then I am sure the pervert will never taste freedom again.

For anyone about to, or thinking about, re-tracing my steps, do not fear a court trial against your abuser. Do not fear an aggressive cross-examination by a Defence Counsel. Do not have any fear because you have two things that your abuser and his court defender do not have... Your most powerful weapons, honesty, and the truth. No amount of slick talking or deflecting tactics can beat that! Throw down that gauntlet!

Several popular and well read, mainstream Scottish newspapers covered the trial, none more so than Scottish Sun reporter Stuart Patterson who had been a great support to me throughout and was in the courtroom during the entire trial and he had been in attendance every day although I did not speak to him until after the trial had ended.

The Scottish Sun wrote…

"Celtic Boys Club predator cast a shadow on my life for 50yrs – I want him to die in jail."

The Celtic Boys Club player whose entire adult life was haunted by Jim Torbett's abuse told how he hopes the depraved paedo dies in jail. Gordon Woods, 68, burst into tears when he discovered a jury had believed him and convicted his ex-coach of a series of monstrous attacks that started when he was just 13 years old and continued for a year.
Jim Torbett was sentenced to another three years in jail It took the dad of three more than 50 years to finally speak up. But he revealed he was desperate to take back control from predator Torbett, who forced him to the brink of suicide. And he made sure he stared the pervert in the eye when he confronted him in court last week.

Gordon, who bravely waived his anonymity, yesterday told The Scottish Sun: "I hope he rots in jail. I want him to die in prison. I hope he is never released because I believe he is still and will always be a danger. Children will never be safe as long as he is on the streets. He is an animal; he is completely evil. There is no other explanation for what he's done. I'm so glad he knows that he doesn't have a single ounce of power over me anymore."

Torbett was convicted of child abuse for the third time after jurors found him guilty of preying on Gordon in 1967.

The indecent assaults went on for more than a year in his car, a flat and a toy shop in Glasgow. Torbett had denied wrongdoing but was nailed after a trial and caged for three years. The former football coach — who founded the boys club in 1966 is already serving a six-year jail term for sex offences against boys. He was locked up in 2018 for abusing three children over eight years, his second conviction for child abuse.

Gordon told how he was desperate to become a footballer but confessed that he couldn't even get a game with his school side. After he flopped in his trial he was amazed when twisted Torbett told him he'd still won a prized place in his boys' club team.

The then trusting schoolboy thought the predator saw potential in him that no one else had. But instead of footie glory, what followed was a year of harrowing abuse that tainted his life and even affected his relationship with his own children.

Gordon said: "Things would probably have turned out differently if I'd never met Jim Torbett. He has cast a shadow over my life for 50 years. When my kids were growing up, I couldn't hug them. I couldn't have them on my knee. I couldn't handle being a father."

Gordon reckons he could have been Torbett's first victim when the coach began attacking him in 1967. He told how the paedo volunteered to drive him home to Drumchapel, Glasgow, but would stop his motor a few hundred yards away from the front door.

The future millionaire businessman would fondle terrified Gordon, perform a sex act on himself and force the lad to touch him.

Gordon told how this happened as many as 40 times. He was also molested during a sleepover at Torbett's high-rise flat after the sicko asked him to wear Celtic Boys Club shorts. And in another attack, he was targeted in the back room of a toy shop in Maryhill, Glasgow.

Gordon revealed he sometimes thinks he was fortunate. He said: "It sounds odd, but I may have been lucky. He hadn't found his confidence when he attacked me. I think I could have been the first boy he abused. I don't know of any before me. As it went on and he was allowed to get away with it he became far more aggressive."

A year later, the abuse stopped when Torbett told Gordon their 'friendship' had to end and ordered him to stay away from training. His life went on to be a rollercoaster for years and he blamed the abuse for his marriage failing.

The tormented dad decided to speak out for the first time in 2019 after he saw Celtic FC were denying a link with the boys' club. He gave a statement to cops and Torbett was eventually quizzed by detectives and charged.

Gordon gave evidence against the paedophile at the High Court in Inverness last week and

came face to face with him for the first time since 1968. He said: "There was going to be a screen, but I told them I didn't want it. I didn't want Torbett to think he had any control over me. I wanted to be eye to eye with him."

The boys club founder appeared to be looking at Gordon as he told the jurors about the sexual abuse.

Gordon said: "I felt him staring at me the whole time I was speaking. But whenever I looked at him, he turned away from me. I felt I'd taken back the power he'd over me for all those years." Gordon described the conviction as "bitter icing on a bitter cake". But his allegations meant that Torbett — in jail for abusing other young players — could not apply for parole. He will now be behind bars for at least another four years.

Gordon said: "The important thing is the court believed me. I've been called all sorts of things and accused of making things up to make money. But the jury believed what I told them. That's vindication that's been a long time coming."

Gordon suffers from stage four lung condition COPD, which damages his lungs, and fears he only has a few years left to live. But he hopes speaking out means others will come forward and ensure Torbett never sees the light of day.

He said: "My life is almost over. But I fear there are other victims out there who are suffering in silence. This conviction shows they should come forward. Don't let Torbett feel like he's got away with what he did to them. As he tries to sleep tonight, he knows he's no longer getting away with what he did to me. That feels really good."

Yesterday, Judge Andrew Cubie told Torbett: "The evidence disclosed a cynical and deliberate targeting and grooming of this boy entirely for your own selfish sexual ends.

"You preyed on his age, dependence, and his concerns about what would happen to the boys club, his confusion and his fear."

I released a press statement as the verdict was announced.

Despite the Defence Advocate KC, deliberately being 'mistaken' in Court several times and trying so hard to blacken my character, I can confirm Mr. James Torbett has been found guilty on all charges. Sentenced to 3 years in prison.

I care not any term of imprisonment he got. Any sentence handed down will only be bitter icing on a tasteless cake. I have secured what I set out to do. A guilty verdict.

I told my story in a court of law. I faced my abuser in court after having requested the screen separating us be removed, I wanted it shown that he no longer had any power over me. It was now my time to take control, I took control; my silence was ended and Torbett is guilty on all 4 counts.

Gordon Woods
25th April 2023

Torbett's Previous Trials…

November 1998.

Abuse of three juvenile players between October 1967 and March 1974, and given a prison sentence of 30 months.

June 2018.

Torbett trial commences, he denied all charges.

July 2018.

Contempt of court order, trial halted.

October 2018.

Torbett went on trial again charged with nine offences of sexual assault on six children between 1970 and 1990.

November 2018.

Found guilty of five offences against three boys and was sentenced to six years in prison.

April 2023.

At the High Court in Inverness. Torbett was found guilty of four charges of sexually abusing Gordon Woods, a player in 1967 and in 1968. Previously potentially eligible for early release in May 2024, he was jailed for a further three years. The additional 3 years only starts when his current jail term ends.

26. CIVIL JUSTICE

There would probably have been no Civil Action if Holyrood, with a cross-party vote, had not recently passed the new Qualified One-Way Cost Shifting Law into statute in Scotland. Without their introduction of this law, each and every claimant would have been compelled to take action separately. This would of course have been prohibitively expensive for the claimants and massively time consuming on the court system.

Not only does it allow all claimants to proceed within the one action it also gives those individuals a sense of belonging to a group, they are no longer a single entity and battling alone, they are all fighting for the same just cause, they are 'The Celtic Claimants Family'.

Of course, with the law being new to the statute, it was imperative that the process and its progress through the court system was meticulous, considering no precedent has ever been set. Judges had to ensure each step of the process was within the boundaries of the new law.

Celtic Football Club of course fights the process in every way they can. Even now, 56 years after being abused by Torbett, Celtic still thinks the abuse insignificant enough to continue abusing me and others, 100's of others. In the 1960's

Torbett abused me and in the 2020's Celtic are continuing to do so without a single thought to its victims whose lives are still being trespassed upon in the most abhorrent way!

Patrick McGuire, the Senior Lawyer for the victims was recently interviewed by The Case Against Celtic Boys' Club Podcast and was unable to hold back his disgust at this world famous, professional sporting organisation, allegedly built on, and its entire fabric revolving around, being a charitable organisation first and a football team second. Nothing could be further from the truth.

"They stand apart from every other defender, every other organisation I have ever pursued a claim against in terms of the way they have thumbed their nose to the survivors of abuse, and it's important to bear in mind the context here, that's what we're talking about, people who were abused as children who are merely seeking financial justice and Celtic have played every trick in the book, have done everything in their power to obfuscate, to delay, to spin, trying to avoid at all cost their moral, and we say legal responsibility to pay compensation to these survivors".

The Case Against Celtic Boys Club Podcast,
Patrick McGuire, Senior Lawyer
Thompson Solicitors 26th June 2023

You must always remember that from 1967 until 1997, the Celtic Football Club, its board of Directors, its supporters, its sponsors, its players, its managers, its backroom staff, and its official Celtic View publication were all proud of Celtic Boys' Club, they were all proud that the Boys' Club was part of the Celtic family. It was only when that very first conviction was made public, and Torbett was sentenced to 2 years for abusing 3 players, 3 children, in 1997 was 'separate entity' born. Since then, until now, Celtic Football Club's response to the now 9 paedophiles with connections to the club being convicted, to the 300+ victims, is nothing short of disgraceful. For any organisation to mock, continue to abuse, and to try every dirty trick in the book to avoid their responsibilities is as abhorrent as the abuse inflicted by the filth who abused the children. Those abusers were given an opportunity, given a free reign, were given a realm within which they could brazenly attack and assault children, both physical and sexually, knowing their horrific deeds were and would be covered up just to 'keep the good name of 'Celtic clean at all times'.

Celtic Football Club have allegedly held three internal inquiries to try and determine exactly what went on at their Boys' Club. Two of those inquiry results have yet to be made public, many years after they were allegedly carried out. The third was referred to in a 'Celtic View' article that contained an obvious direct threat to those that were speaking out. No evidence of any remorse, any regret, any concern, just a threat to the consequences on offer, should their victims not shut up, once and for all.

A SUNDAY newspaper recently carried a story which cast a shadow over the Celtic Boys' Club in general, and some of the leaders in particular. It also contained a clear inference that the Celtic Football Club had not taken appropriate action with regard to the allegations contained in the article. In actual fact, the Celtic Board investigated the rumours and interviewed the men concerned in-depth and could find nothing to substantiate the stories that were being circulated. During the course of the last ten days Celtic Football Club and the Boys' Club have been in receipt of hundreds of letters and phone calls from boys and their parents, past and present, stating their complete support and backing of all involved with the Boys' Club. It must be clearly emphasised that apart from this newspaper article, inspired by the former chairman of the Boys' Club, not one single complaint has been received by any other person with a Celtic connection. These Boys' Club leaders who have been placed under a cloud as a result of these rumours have instructed their lawyers to take the appropriate course of action, and if necessary, go to court of law to make sure these scurrilous stories are buried once and for all.

Why any organisation would have 3 inquiries into another, that had nothing to do with them, no connection, no inextricable linkage, indeed were allegedly 'separate entities', evades me. Many of the convictions of Celtic Boys' Club officials and Celtic Football Club employees related to horrific incidents of child abuse after that date. Hundreds, if not thousands of innocent young boys who were in obvious danger, were welcomed into Celtic Boys' Club after that date!

Those abusers were given thirty years, three decades, to abuse, unabated, collectively and in tandem, they attacked many hundreds of victims and brought the horror to countless families. Children's minds were assaulted and lost, wives lost their husbands, parents lost their child, siblings lost their sibling, friends lost their mate, children lost their father. There is no end to the damage they allowed to happen.

Celtic Football Club were, and still are, attempting to cover up its alleged horrific involvement. It must not succeed; it must be made to accept and apologise for its behaviour. It will be shortly when the civil case hits the Court of Session in Edinburgh. I'm confident the court will rule "They knew then, they know now".

Collins dictionary definition of separate entity is certainly revealing…

*If one thing is **separate** from another, there is a barrier, space, or division between them, so that they are clearly two things. An **entity** is something that exists separately from other things and has a clear identity of its own.*

… As far as Celtic Football Club and Celtic Boys' Club are concerned 'separate entity' is a nonsense, and it is an affront to the Judicial system that, that is the reasoning behind Celtic Football Club's so strenuously contesting the class-action and heaping further abuse, stress, and confusion on its victims.

As I write the Civil Class Action is ongoing with the next anticipated hearing in a few months' time. That will hear whether or not Celtic can receive a fair trial in consideration of the time that has lapsed since the abuse was prevalent.

Celtic are citing a previous case where it was deemed in court that the defenders could not receive a fair trial, this case however involved an action where the perpetrators had all died, where there had been no complaints to the police and where there had been no convictions. In the Celtic case none of this applies because there have been many convictions, an abundance of records regarding many allegations of abuse being reported to the police and most importantly, most of the perpetrators are still alive.

It is probably Celtic's very last effort to delay these proceedings, but a day will come, very soon, when they will have no option other than to face their victims within a court of law.

That day is a day Celtic's victim have been seeking, desperately, for over fifty years.

It's coming, for every victim, every family.

27. WHERE I AM NOW

Where am I now after having made the decision to come forward after 50 years of silence? I'm in a relatively good place considering the upheaval in my life coming forward has introduced.

Writing this book has been very difficult. I have had to prepare myself many times to put to paper the most personal issues of my life. I have cried, many times, lost my composure, many times, lost patience with all around me, including my beautiful little baby girl, undeservedly, many times. I've fought through it all though as every single victim of the Celtic's Boys' Club deserves my story to be told and put in the public domain. Why? Because my story is their story too. Read every word I have written and understand 100's of young boys could write the exact same words with regards to how the abuse affected them and their innocent families.

I've opened up too many, millions perhaps, and hopefully, my words will demonstrate how hard that has been. But believe me, every tear I've shed since I came forward and in writing this book, has been in honour of those who can't, whether that be through misplaced shame, guilt, fear of not being believed, or the many who have passed before they could muster their courage to do so. For whatever reason they have not, or cannot, come forward, I honour them and their memory.

Yes, it has been emotional, it has been hard, and it has certainly been eventful, but do you know what? I'm glad I decided to 'do the right thing'. If my coming forward helps to ease the suffering of any one individual, gives others the strength to speak out and get support, or assist in any small way in getting the justice all victims deserve then it has been a journey I am so glad I took.

I have many great memories of my life looking back. Everything I have had till now, relationships, children, careers, travel, failures, and successes have fatefully followed what happened as a child. Without those early events, my life would have been totally different. With the abuse removed and distanced, I am still satisfied with the memories I do have and what I have achieved. Those great memories should allow me now to look back at them with pride and a satisfaction that I did as best as I could, as I near my last leg in life and to be thankful for everything. I can with a few, but the others don't allow me to do so. All my great memories come with a shadow attached, I'd rather they didn't, but they do, I have to accept that and not allow those shadows to destroy my past life completely.

You will now hopefully understand from my story that the abuse these perpetrators dish out doesn't only destroy young lives at the point of abuse. The effect of their actions last years, decades, lifetimes. Not only to the abused individuals themselves but also all those close to them for the rest of their lives. How a human being can justify, in any way, doing that to a child is impossible to understand. I cannot come to terms with it. My whole life has been affected negatively by what happened to me and my family.

My only regret in my actions is that I have had to involve my surviving family in all these disclosures. One brother and one sister have sadly passed without learning of my young sadness, that's maybe a good thing. My other siblings were approached after many years of silence and no contact to prepare them for the press and TV reports that were about to expose my story. My own children, friends, neighbours, even work colleagues were prepared also and it was very difficult for them and myself to accept all that happened. Most have been very understanding and supportive, most didn't know just what to say, I understand that, and respect their silences. They would all have been better not knowing, and just innocently ignoring what I went through, I didn't give them that opportunity and I hope they understand why?

Coming forward has also given me the opportunity to meet many brave people especially Bill Storrie and Martin Rodgers who appeared with me on the Alex Thomson report on Channel 4. I thank Alex on behalf of victims in bringing this to the eyes and ears of the public. I had approached many people within the media and Government to help with making my story and experiences known. They spoke a lot but said absolutely nothing. They listened a lot but heard absolutely nothing. It seemed I was on my own other than a select few who it would appear were able to put their morals before their own agendas.

Also, thanks again to Keith McLeod at the Daily Record for his/their support in highlighting my own individual story as well as the stories of many others, many others who are hopefully soon going to get the justice they so rightly deserve. I doubt I could have taken the steps I have without the support of Keith and his organisation.

A mention too for Henry McDonald from The Guardian who came to see me in the February of 2020. He travelled up from London to interview me which subsequently led to his 4 page 'Long Read' report in October 2020. I was recently advised that the on-line readers of this report had recently passed 4 million readers world-wide. Henry sadly passed in early 2023 and he was always there in the background offering his appreciated support. He intended to follow up his story on any convictions and on the Class Action underway against Celtic. He was denied that opportunity.

Huge thanks to Sonia Poulton who supported me by allowing me a lengthy interview with her to tell my story on a Raw Report Special and her subsequent interviews on RISE to update her and her viewers on my fight for justice.

And a massive thanks to Emma-Jane Taylor who contributed through a Chapter (Page196) on her Charity Project 90/10 **#notmyshame** that indicates routes to help those in need of support. Emma-Jane also wrote the Foreword to this book.

In recent years the Scottish Daily Express and The Scottish Sun have started to take an interest and began to intermittently report on the Celtic Boys Club Scandal. Of course, I thank them for being there now and doing their part in opening their readers eyes to all that has gone on, but must ask them where have they been for the past 50 years? Only now, when myself and others like me have given them their stories on a plate do they take advantage of our hard work, our fight, our determination, and fearless approach, without any remorse it appears for remaining silent for so many years. We had to fight, and fight hard, without their help when we needed it, for them to waltz in and write their stories and give themselves a pat on the back. Where were your investigative journalists when we really needed you? In fairness, the Daily Record, The Scottish Daily Express and latterly The Scottish Sun have all been there for me and wrote articles about my own individual case throughout the past 4 years. But that's not the issue, my individual case was a very small part of the history of the Celtic family. Whereas reports were published on individual criminal cases regularly the enormous elephant in the room, that being the Celtic Football Club's involvement has been largely ignored, it should not have been. I will continue to shout, and shout loud, to ensure they answer their victim's questions in a court of law and those questions and answers are recorded, widely, globally, in print.

The Scottish Government also must be acknowledged, as without their understanding and support of victims and survivors of child abuse throughout society, and their families, they would not have recently passed two very important areas into Scots Law that made many of these convictions, and indeed, the civil action to have been possible. Firstly, Limitation (Childhood Abuse) (Scotland) Act 2017 removed the 3-year limitation in bringing criminal actions against perpetrators when the abuse took place when the victim was a child. Secondly, the introduction of Qualified One-Way Cost Shifting that allows group proceedings to be brought against organisations who have questions to answer. Without those major changes to the law in Scotland justice would have been denied too so many.

Important for me to say though that Torbett hasn't won. I had imagined the filthy bastard sitting and revelling in his past crimes. Thinking of his victims, I got away with that one, and that one, and that one too. I am now satisfied that when he tries to sleep and he thinks of me now he will have to accept, I didn't get away with that one, he will spend an additional 3 long years thinking I didn't get away with that one!

Currently, I am a resident of Scotland, in a small, quiet village where I run my small business from home. From my window, I can see trees, fields, and the innocence of farm animals. I have been here now for 10 years after spending some time living in the Midlands, South of England, Russia and the far-East. I am settled and very happy. I live very near to my first two, now adult, children and see them often. Perhaps our relationship can be strained at times but then again isn't everyone's?

I have now retired and in receipt of my pensions. I still work, part-time though because I want to. I love what I do and without my work, I would spend my day with too many memories. Running the business dictates I have always to look to my tomorrows, not my yesterdays.

Thirteen years, ago at the age of 55, I found myself the single father of a delightful, beautiful, 10-month-old baby girl. I had options of course but I chose to dedicate my time going forward in securing the best possible future for my baby daughter. For the past thirteen years, that's exactly what I've done. I have had no relationships in that time. No helping hand, and no domestic support, I've managed without. The only thing I have missed, to be honest, is the occasional cuddle, the warmth of a close friend, and the companionship a partner can bring. Mostly though I miss the assurance from an adult someone to tell me that everything is going to be all right. I put all those negatives out of my mind and concentrate only on ensuring my little-one is happy and safe.

On my own, decisions have been made, my story told, now I can tell myself everything is going to be all right and believe it! I firmly believe my decision to come forward has helped. It has helped to right some of the wrongs that have been forced onto our children for decades.

One of the greatest moments in this journey was when the Channel 4 report aired on TV. My daughter, then 10-years-old sat with me to watch. She was aware, of course, of the story but not the intricacies. She had been told that a bad man did bad things to me when I was a little boy and played for Celtic. She accepted that and hasn't, so far, asked for further details. Unexpectedly when I appeared on screen, I actually became quite emotional. I managed to control it, but a tear fell, and my little one noticed. She asked if I was OK and when I replied in the affirmative, she leaned over, kissed my cheek, and whispered: "I'm so proud of you Daddy". That, in itself, made my questionable decision to announce my own individual story, and to start on my journey, rewarding far and beyond any of my prior expectations.

Before I go a special thanks to all the pathetic haters on social media. Those sick trolls that tried everything in their power to ridicule, mock, demean, frustrate, call me a phony, a gold-digger, and tried desperately to 'keep the good name of Celtic clean at all times'… the bastards failed! Your trolling ensured the cultivation of my determination and each insult directed at me was fuel for my campaign, fuel for my positive state of mind and fuel for my continuance to go on and see justice against my abuser and his enablers, in my eyes, Celtic Football Club.

I recently stated in a press interview that if I had known four years ago, what I know now, I would still have come forward but would have possibly not waived my anonymity. I've been thinking about that, and do you know what? I wouldn't change a thing. That waiver gave hundreds, perhaps thousands of those sad, unsavoury, excuses for human beings the opportunity to try and force me to stop and to shut my mouth with their constant attacks on social media. Even after Torbett's conviction, in April of 2023, incredibly, the attacks continued, 'keep the good name of Celtic clean at all times' was the only thing on their minds. No empathy, no sympathy for the children abused, despite those kids being lovers of the same club, despite those kids, at one point, having proudly pulled on the Hoops and represented Celtic Football Club's Boys' Club.

They wanted me back in my box, to send me to an abyss, the same box that Torbett and Celtic Football Club put me in and sealed all those years ago. So no, I would again waive my anonymity with pride because that decision gave me the power, that decision made sure that I could never stop, never shut up, never let them get away with their abhorrence without a court of law listening to me.

They should all be extremely proud of themselves as they all played their part in convicting James Torbett, and they will all have played their part in ensuring Celtic Football Club is held to account. Thank you so much Trolls, you know who you are, your help was sincerely appreciated.

I'll sign off now with a sincere thank you for taking the time to read my most secret secrets. They are no longer secrets of course. I have opened my life to possibly millions by waiving my anonymity via, the written media, T.V., the courts, social media, and now of course, this book. I just hope that not one of those millions who have been invited to consider my story, regardless of religion, club affiliations, nationality, race, or gender feel that they can condone, cover-up or excuse what has happened to our children, your children! Not just at that club, but many clubs, from many countries throughout the world. Not just at football clubs either because child abuse is rampant in all walks of life. It must be addressed, and it must be stopped as best that we, as a society can. The authorities must make the punishment severe enough to ensure the filth fear it and keep their abusing hands to themselves and well distanced from little children. No more soft sentences, no more slaps on the wrist, no more trying to 'understand' the abusers. No more!

It's important to me that I inform the reader how abuse is not just something that happens to the victims as kids. The abuse lingers with us forever. Many of the chapters in the book have tried to get that across and show you how the abuse I suffered at the hands of the deviant Torbett affected everything in my life for my whole life. I hope I managed to get that message across and give the reader a better understanding of what the child abuse consequences are. Many people are so far unaware of that fact. They advise 'to move on and forget it as it was 20 years ago', hopefully now they will better understand why a surviving victim cannot just move on, it's not an option.

I have used the term victim a lot throughout this book. Many individuals do not like that term and prefer to be called survivors. Sorry, but I don't agree. To me 'survivor' is just a way of cleansing the word 'victim,' trying to make it less controversial, more acceptable in discussion, and an effort to minimise the crimes committed on children. I will never allow my story, my history nor my experience, at the hands of a paedophile, be cleansed. Let's call it what it is, paedophilia, paedophiles who create victims who then become survivors. Yes, we are all survivors, we've survived being victims of paedophilia, something no child should ever have to deal with.

There is something that I need to make very clear. Now that you have read instances of the sadness and the bad times my abuse had brought to me there is another side to that coin. I have had, overall, a very happy life, with some great memories and many things to be thankful for. Some very deep, meaningful relationships over the years, 3 beautiful children, and success in my professional career, I've seen a great deal of our world, having completed my world tour as a 16-year-old, worked and lived in Russia for 6 months, and 7 years living and working in the far-East, and strange as it seems wouldn't want to change a thing. To have all those wonderful things in my life, the abuse I endured was just one element in my path to achieving those. It wasn't all sad, I've only told you about those as that is what this book is all about. Today I'm in my 70th year and I am happy, content, and looking forward to many more years with my wonderful children and can enjoy my last few remaining years free of campaigning, free of fear, and free of an ever-darkening cloud over me, it's nice to breathe again.

I have no political allegiances, or club allegiances, no reason to pursue my cause for any reason other than justice for everyone who has suffered, children at the hands of these animals. The perpetrators of child sexual abuse should never see the light of day to abuse again, and their enablers, all those who turned a blind eye, all those who knew exactly what was going on but stayed silent, should accompany them, safely and securely, behind bars.

More convictions to follow?

Criminal Justice served 25th April 2023

Civil Justice expected in 2024.

28. A HERO

Throughout this book I have made reference to a gentleman who gave testimony at the Torbett trial in April of 2023 on behalf of the prosecution.

It was my aim, one day, to meet him after 55 years and thank him for all that he bravely chose to do to ensure Torbett was found guilty, I wanted to look him in the eyes and to shake his hand.

I was aware that he was not in the best of health and that his evidence was heard via a video link.

He was in the car when Torbett threw me out the club unceremoniously, so his evil abhorrence's could continue unabated.

A few weeks prior to the publication of this book and less than two months after the trial I received the terribly sad news that he had passed away.

I didn't get the chance to thank him personally, but he knew the importance of his testimony and he knew what it meant to me and to others.

This true gentleman was instrumental, no, his testimony was imperative and without it there was little chance of a conviction.

I will be forever grateful to him, and his family

should be proud of the man their father was.

Despite his own worries, he put others first and re-lived his experience at the hands of Torbett after having done so, in court, once before in 1997.

His family have asked that I do not mention him by name. A request I will of course respect.

I know who he was, his family knows who he was, and I end by raising a glass to a wonderful true gentleman.

Thank you.

Rest In Peace My Friend.

Thank you again for your support.

Enjoy your football kids!

Memorial
Rosemary Woods • Passed 27.11.97.
James Woods • Passed 16.12.97.

*Thanks to my children who supported me throughout my
disclosures, that support was instrumental in my success.
Craig Woods, Victoria Woods, Briana (Kanna) Woods*
"Nothing is out of your reach".

Anyone seeking advice on taking those first steps to come forward are directed to Chapter 24 (page 200) where help contacts are available.

Media reports over the years...

The Case Against Celtic Boys Club Podcast.
The Daily Record Breaks The Story.
Alex Thomson • **Channel 4 Documentary.**
Sonia Poulton • **The Raw Report Special.**
Adrian Goldberg • **The Celtic Boys Club Scandal.**
Ed Opperman • **Interviews - USA.**
Gary Johnson • **Interviews - Australia.**
The Guardian 4-page Pull-out - October 2020.
Westminster To Get Involved? - January 2022.
Scottish Government In Hiding? - January 2022.
Celtic Lawsuit Given Go Ahead – March 2022.
Overseas Abuse - January 2023.
Gordon Woods • **Taking Back Control - April 2023.**

Gordon Woods on Twitter - @GordonW09225415
on Facebook - /BeingPutThroughHoops

Links to these and others, can be followed by visiting... www.beingputthroughhoops.co.uk

Printed in Great Britain
by Amazon